You love to rebel, provoke and cause some agitation.

You have a stirring that is quietly burning, gathering knowledge and experience and knows that one day – some day real soon - you will be ready to reveal that special quiet, yet powerful, energy.

You need help if you are dragging on that grey 'Con Belt', and to offer, inspire and suggest alternative ideas and solutions to jump off and create that Nourishing and Flourishing life.

You need encouragement to express your artistic talents, on video, stage or page by learning from the experiences and reactions of those that just did it or are still involved in showbiz.

You want to re-learn and revise your natural performance skills to accomplish and achieve whatever you want in life. It is about putting performance back into your vocabulary in a positive way.

You thought you could, or think you can Step Up & Stand Out and just need more encouragement, some confidence boosting and a sense that you are not alone.

You feel you have it in you, believe you can do it or feel you are so close and yet have 'buts and ifs' hanging like old wrinkled carrots in front of you - the 'so close but so far' scenario.

You believe that there is gold in that river, a brilliant opportunity in sight or a stage to stand on with an audience of thousands and you want to feel part of something, want to Stand Out.

You want to do something different, want to share your original spirit and have an urge to change the world.

THIS BOOK WILL HELP YOU:

Understand how you can learn to be confident and courageous and then go out and perform competently.

Show you that your performance skills are your indispensible key to achievement and success.

I hope you enjoy the journey we will take together. If you want to **Step Up & Stand Out** – then THIS BOOK IS FOR YOU.

Georgia Varjas 2019

REVIEWS

Georgia Varjas nails it in this passionate commentary on female empowerment and performance. Written in a lively and accessible style, spicily seasoned with the author's personal stories, The Rule Breaker's Guide is a confidence booster and for any woman stepping into public life. Drawing upon a lifetime's experience of taking risks and following her dreams, Varjas shows us how feistiness, authenticity and a willingness to learn can liberate us and transform social conventions.

Sally Gillespie, PhD.
Author of 'Living the Dream' and the 'Book of Dreaming'.

This book isn't so much a breath of fresh air as a veritable tornado! Georgia shares her own wisdom, wins and woes to shine a light on how the rules can hold us back, keep us small, and shut us up when we don't have to let them. With a combination of story and sass, Georgia shows us how to ditch the status quo and be mistresses of our own lives. And she plays with words like a pro (which she is), so it's a joy to read. Compulsory reading!

Gayle Johnson, Copy Writer and Writing Mentor.

In this powerful anthem on how to step up and stand out, author Georgia Varjas not only inspires through her powerful and sometimes cheeky storytelling, but also redefines authenticity, empowerment and what it means to be a woman and own our worth.

Tricia Brouk – Award-winning director, writer, filmmaker and the Executive Producer of Speakers Who Dare.

The Rule Breaker's Guide is a breathless journey through the trials of women trying to reach the top (or just anywhere near the top, thank-you!) but letting ourselves and our societal expectations get in the way.

Georgia Varjas is our guide throughout and brings her experience from the world of showbiz as a musician and world-renowned poet to highlight how a woman's challenge to live her best life has not gone away just because it's 2019; we need to work harder than ever to ensure that we are seen and heard.

Georgia is more than aware of the challenges that 'being you' brings and so provides advice, steps and philosophies to help bring out the courage to live our best lives in this time of #MeToo and unequal pay. Her stories and examples, although at times painful to read, will have you marveling at how amazing us women are at getting back up again, and again, and again, in times of adversity.

Backed up by quotes and references from some of the best minds on the planet, this isn't just Georgia's story, but the story for all women – and men. We need to keep telling these tales as all the while we fight for true equality, whilst being our most fabulous selves along the way.

Vicki Jakes, Director, Way Out Far

ACKNOWLEDGEMENTS

Praise and thanks go out to the many women and men who contributed and supported me during this book-ride roller-coaster, and indeed, in my life.

I have always preferred to work in a team; nothing like pooling the talents and skills of a group and creating some genius and magic. Writing a book requires one pen - my pen - but also the influences and wisdom of those around me.

Credit goes out to the people with whom I discussed, deliberated and debated all the topics in my book.

Also, to the books and articles I read that spurred me to write more, that urged me to dig deeper.

I want to thank those that read and reviewed the book, who generously gave their time, energy and heart to sharing their opinions and thoughts.

To Sally Gillespie, whom I hadn't seen in more than thirty years and yet didn't hesitate to write a most glorious review.

To Gayle Johnson, a writing mentor with extraordinary intuitive and intelligent skills.

To Vicki Jakes, a multi-skilled woman, a digital queen, a mother of two gorgeous girls and a real feminist juggler.

To Tricia Brouk, with whom I had just two short conversations and knew immediately, with her vast experience and talent in the show-biz world, would be an excellent woman to write a review.

To Harriet Waley-Cohen who also generously shared her impressions and feminine intuitive wisdom in writing the Foreword for my book.

To the lovely Olivia Eisinger, who witnessed all my misplaced commas and colons, deleted my bad spelling and sometimes dodgy word order.

To Chris Day, who challenged me to write the book in 4 months and I did it in 3 months, two weeks and sprinkling of hours!

To all the team at Filament.

To the right-on sisters at Literally PR, Helen and Diana and all the Girls behind the scenes.

To Lorraine Pannetier, who wrote beautiful words for my bio with her soulful and magical pen.

Much love and appreciation goes to Joy and Eric Lennick for their continuing support and joie de vivre.

To Anna Friewald, who, without even realising it, gave me great support and love when I needed it.

To my sweetheart nieces, Lara and Natalie Khoo, who continue to inspire me.

To Natalie and James Smith, my V.A and video team, (respectively) who have followed and recorded this journey with me with much attention, care and warmth.

And huge special love and thanks to Gyula Friewald, my soulmate forever. Who offered me incredible insights, inspirations and wild vocabulary throughout my book-ride roller-coaster.

Much thanks and praise to all the amazing women who shared their points of view and experiences.

And to the army of Boys (big, small and in-between) I met during my wonderful years in the show-biz world who gave me fuel and fire.

And to all those who shared words of kindness and love, those strangers with whom I did not exchange names or any other details, just warmth and humanity. Thank you.

The tongue has no bones, but it is strong enough to break a heart. Be careful with your words, take care of your language.

Anon (who obviously was a woman)

Georgia Varjas May 2019

THE RULE BREAKER'S GUIDE

TO STEP UP & STAND OUT

A MANIFESTO FOR REBELS

GEORGIA VARJAS

Published by
Filament Publishing Ltd.
16 Croydon Road, Beddington
Croydon, Surrey, CR0 4PA, United Kingdom
www.filamentpublishing.com
Telephone: +44 (0)208 688 2598

ISBN 978-1-913192-18-1
Printed by 4edge Ltd.

The right of Georgia Varjas to be recognised as the author of this work has been asserted by her in accordance with the Designs and Copyright Act 1988.

CONTENTS

FOREWORD

*And one day she discovered that she was fierce,
and strong, and full of fire, and that not even she
could hold herself back because her passion burned
brighter than her fears.*

Mark Anthony, *The Beautiful Truth*

Buckle up. Prepare to be woken up to the realities of a world in which being a successful woman is not easy as it should be.

The uncomfortable truth is that despite progress in equality, there is a hell of a long way to go. Culture and unconscious programming for many men and women remain stuck in patriarchal ways, and this is stacked against women.

In The Rule Breaker's Guide, Georgia has laid out razor sharp insights about the barriers and problems that persist for women. Her understanding of why they are there, from religion, politics and cultural evolution - is deeply knowledgeable and compelling. Pointing out these contributors to the lack of confidence many women suffer is necessary, if provocative and uncomfortable at times. Georgia's personal stories illuminate the issues with humour; the truth is they are wake-up calls to those that deny the problems persist, partly because they are so relatable. If you haven't experienced the same or similar yourself, you sure as hell know a woman who has.

This book is a call to arms. Its message is a wake-up call about what it will take for things to be different. In my view, The Rule Breaker's Guide is just as important for men as it is for women. All men should be feminists, and if actions speak louder than words, they need to behave differently too. Men must stop taking advantage of the privilege they have enjoyed up until now if they truly want equality, for women to be confident and reach their potential, and for society to reap the benefits of having women run the show just as much, if not more, than men.

In my work, where I empower women to believe in themselves and their potential, one of the guiding principles I teach is that of leaving behind victim, powerless mode in favour of radical personal responsibility for your life, state of mind, fulfilment and wellbeing.

Nothing will change unless you go out and make it happen. It takes courage of course, as Georgia so rightly points out. Saying 'no' to the man who wants access to your body in return for a promotion is just as important as who you vote for in terms of standing up and being counted - being the change you want to see in the world. With courageous actions comes greater confidence, and more courageous actions follow, thus sowing the seeds for a very different path for the future.

The Rule Breaker's Guide offers an abundance of concise, clear advice about how take personal responsibility for getting where you want to be, how to be courageous, to find your confidence and your voice. There is no doubt in my mind that for society to break free from the patriarchal paradigm and for women to shine and contribute as they should, change is needed from the bottom up as well as the top down.

Notice the rules that are stacked against you, and that society suffers when you stick to them. Don't play that old game. Step Up. Break the rules. Take responsibility for creating the life and society you want, and know you have a very important part to play in the rules of the future.

Harriet Waley Cohen
May 2019

INTRODUCTION

I have a black and white photo of me as a baby, bouncing up and down in my playpen/cot. I am holding onto the sides gurgling a tune, a gleeful smile stretched across my plump baby cheeks – and my nappy is full – like really full!

My mother most definitely heard me, for sure understood me and had no problem in believing in me.

You could say it was the beginning of my deep female wisdom that to be heard, understood and believed, you had to make an impact, an impression.

In my life, I have had many experiences where being heard, understood and believed never happened, or didn't bring the results I expected. But that is how I learnt - from making mistakes. All those boo-boos, slip-ups and errors showed me feedback, and I learnt I wasn't perfect and didn't have to be either. Rather, I am wise and experienced – those delicious feminine skills.

School bored me so much that I had turned into a cheeky rebel by the time I was 10. My school reports sighed, begging me to concentrate and focus. But I couldn't pay any attention or waste my energy on 1066 and all that warmongering.

I left home when I was 15 – but hey relax, I didn't go to jail, rehab or any other custodial institution! I attended a sixth-form college and attempted three A-levels while working to pay for rent and food.

I cleaned toilets; in fact, I got a job cleaning the toilets in my own college. I'd crawl into the building at 6 am and whizz round the WC facilities giving them a swipe and a mop. By 7.30, I was done and done in. I found a quiet corner in the girls' changing rooms and slept till the students drifted in around 9 am.

In the evenings after college, I worked in a hair treatment clinic, massaging bald men's heads and applying lotions and potions to make their hair grow. If they got fresh with me, by leaning their heads back to lie on my bosom, I turned up the heat and speed on the massage machine.

After that, conventional work, straight work or doing the '9 to 5' never ever entered my head. By the time I reached 18, I had enough of working to a timetable and doing something I hated just to please others - read men! After all, I had been fending for myself for several years and I knew I couldn't take this kind of exploitation any more.

Years of non-stimulus at school and college made me determined to get off that 'Con Belt' (Conveyer Belt). There had to be another way to survive, to make money, to express myself, to travel and see the world and then make plenty more money.

You see, I learnt the value of money early. Living in one room with my sister and parents for the first five years of my life, I learnt to love and appreciate space. Having to work to pay the rent and feed myself during my teenage years showed me the real value of what a decent wage should be. Yes, I wanted more money to live in better conditions and live a life – a Nourishing and Flourishing life.

Of course, I had many struggles, rejections and hard times. I had days when I had no money and would go and steal potatoes from an allotment nearby. I had days when I didn't have any buzz or energy to go out hunting and hustling. I had many lonely times when I felt abandoned and unloved. But somehow in my gut, my strong feminine instinct pulled me through those desperate periods.

I have had many adventures in the Show- Biz world. I turned my hand, heart and creative energy and applied myself to a variety of art forms.

The book reveals some stories of my days in the music business, in theatre and on the Spoken Word scene. There will be more, in another book.

One of the big lessons I learnt from all my escapades on this crazy spinning earth is that if you don't Step Up & Stand Out in your own unique way and Perform to your best ability – rain or shine – you will be stuck on that Con Belt for life.

The word 'performance' has had a bad press for many decades (centuries) but for me, it is clear it means the way you express yourself to the world. It is your choice of words, style and movement. It is your decision to design the shape, shade and colour of your entry into any type of work you want to do.

Performing with all your heart, mind and skills to show - boss, orchestra, producer, banker, doctor, professor, CEO, client, massive, 2,000-strong audience – what you are made of. What you are **really** made of.

In my opinion, an authentic performance or performing authentically is one and the same thing. They are sisters, not broiling divas. They are compatible. They work and design together. They are the essence of you, the creative energy that you articulate in your own unique way.

This motif is at the heart of my book. This is the belly of my philosophy. To find the courage and confidence to create the life you want. To develop and learn about your creative skills, artistic abilities, passionate imagination, visionary ideas - call it what you may - your inventiveness even, and go out there and Perform.

• Believe you can do it.
• Disarm your critics.
• Dismiss the negative whisperers.

Because there are obstacles out there.

There are mountains to climb and roller coasters to navigate. From casting couches, glass and bamboo ceilings and all those pinnacles of power and privilege that will stand in your way.

This book strides through those couches, ceilings and concrete pillars, sharing experiences and wisdom from myself and many famous and infamous women as well as some men.

There are examples that offer solutions or at least ways that worked at the time! Some examples can only offer humour as a way to deal with some of the ongoing, deeply imbedded and institutionalised misogyny.

As Greta Thunberg, the Swedish 16-year-old who is a political activist working to stop global warming and climate change, says:

"You are never too small to make a difference."

I am a person, a woman that sees my cup as most definitely half full. There is always another day, another page and another stage to mount and ride. And, I do believe that every time you give the best of yourself, you perform authentically.

Finding your fulfilment through expressing your unique performance skills in any form you wish, is something I encourage. Having re-invented myself many times, I know you can do it, and I know that it brings extraordinary fulfilment.

The book talks about gender politics and the obstacles from history (Her-lack-of-story), including ancestral heritage and downright insulting misogyny. If you don't believe it exists – then read on, baby. If you feel it is changing, you will not be shocked at the continuing injustice and harassment of women and girls. And if you, like myself and many women, want to do something about it, then read on – I have some suggestions.

Above all, this book is about encouraging you to Step Up & Stand Out in whatever it is you want to do in your life.

Have babies or not have babies. Create a multi-million-dollar business and employ all the poor women in Honduras. Become the next female president of the USA, Russia, Saudi or Japan. Start a revolution to end all wars...

For all of these pursuits, you will need confidence, courage, competence and a whole bucket load of personality to perform on this magnificent scale. This book has some of those ingredients. It has data and information to make your blood boil so you will want to Step Up & Make A Difference. It has stories to learn from; after all, mistakes are nothing but feedback. It carries a spirit of 'together we can make change happen'.

This is my story but it is also the story of millions of women and girls around the world. This book is to provoke and encourage you to recognise you can do something wonderful in your life – and make positive changes. I know you will feel my passion, understand my urgency and be entertained by my stories.

Georgia Varjas 2019

CHAPTER ONE:
I WANT TO BE AUTHENTIC!

The Club of Authenticity

Like an aroma of café or sweet chocolate drifting in the air, everyone wants to inhale the essence of being authentic.

The deep desire, almost desperate ambition to be viewed as authentic is taking a grip on the world around us.

In business and relationships, the 'A' word is bounded around like a password to open all doors. It's like a weapon of introduction, inclusion and tribe membership.

It is the new and old buzzword to be part of a gathering, club or group. If you are authentic come in and join us.

Derived from the Greek for 'self' and 'to do or be', authentic means 'to be one's self', and today we use the word when we want to describe being genuine, acting on one's own authority, or possessing an immutable truth.

It amazes me and honestly bothers me too, how people believe that being authentic is being different from who they are now. All day long, we are being ourselves, in all the different roles, disguises and activities we perform.

As Carl Jung reminds us:
"We meet ourselves time and time again in a thousand disguises in our path in life."

Your behaviour changes as new, familiar and old situations arise in your daily life.

Put aside masks, false-hoods, make-up, pretenders, liars and their sidekicks; most of us go around being authentic all the time.

I believe that the reason we crave to be seen as authentic is, in reality, the yearning to overcome the shyness, self-consciousness, and constraints of society.

The longing to be recognised as authentic is like a rebellion from the insecurity and inhibitions of the cultural and religious kind. Those written and un-written laws that hold us back and stop us from expressing what we think, how we feel and in turn, our true opinions.

What I call 'the rules from schools' and the laws and commandments, duties and obligations that bring on this fear of showing your unique personality.

Cultural programming that reaches back thousands of years. Centuries of oppression and suppression accepted and imprinted into our psyche. Dark times when punishments of torture and death were dished out for making herbal teas, as with the witch-hunts of the Middle Ages.

Like the laws that stopped and prevented huge numbers of the population from access to education. Laws that said professions such as judges, neurosurgeons, pilots, presidents and owners of financially successful businesses should not be in the hands of certain sections of society.

No wonder so many people strive 'to be authentic'. No wonder it has become a quest and a pursuit to re-claim the rights and privileges afforded to some but not everyone. I understand this drive and longing to re-gain those arenas previously forbidden or prohibited. It is one hundred percent logical to want to have the same rights and access to life as anyone else.

And what many of us do not realise is that being authentic is part of our daily performance.

The way you are, your mannerisms, gestures, language skills and awareness - all of these indices - contribute to your authentic performance. It includes sticking up for yourself. Stating and saying your terms and conditions in a clear voice. Almost like your personal manifesto of all the things you will and won't do. Performance and authenticity are part of the same package. They are not competitors. They live inside of you - they are both you. The battle you face is not between authenticity and performance, it is the struggle to fight off the indoctrinations, cultural stamps and stigmas of the world as we know it.

Anna Friewald, Horticulturist and Psychonaut:

When I meet a man for the first time or on the first date, I am always clear about what I do and don't do in a relationship. I tell them straight up things like 'I don't shave certain areas.' 'I don't wear thongs and I don't dress up because I have enough roles as it is.' If they can't handle it then, they won't later.

The Residues of Restrictions

How can you release yourself from a millennium of restrictions, physical, emotional and spiritual? Where do you start when we hardly recognise them today? And seldom give them any importance or shrug them off as, 'well that's life!'

Awareness and action comes to my mind. And it starts with a little Her-story, when I try to comprehend the restrictions my mother, grandmother and her ancestors lived through. All the things that were forbidden to them like owning houses, businesses, bank accounts and their own bodies. With that vision our progress is truly amazing.

But I think we need to disturb and agitate the programming much more. Looking at the multitude of rules and laws that still exist and prohibit us from being who we want to be. The difficulties we face in participating in leadership roles, balanced representation at all the decision-making tables, the challenges of motherhood, stigma and criminalization of sex work, equal pay and many other relevant and important issues.

It is about refusing to accept categories. The dangerous ones like being virgin, mother or whore or even maiden, mother and crone, or any of the other categories that subtly define us such as witch, slut or slag. The definitions that suggest we should just accept things as they are when we have children, a profession, a mortgage and responsibility. Definitions that tell us when we reach a certain age, we must and we should have accomplished marriage, children; or be finished with certain things - and we should now keep a low profile.

Changes have happened and massive progress has been made. Laws have been included but few implemented. Let's take a look at the gender pay gap – the difference between average gross hourly earnings of male and female employees.

In the UK in 2016, according to Eurostat, there was a 21% difference in pay between women and men. In the EU as a whole, it was 16.2%. Only Estonia, the Czech Republic and Germany had a wider gap than the UK. The figures have changed little since 2008.

The European Commissioner in charge of equality, Věra Jourová, said she was disappointed the gap between male and female earnings was stagnating across the EU, despite efforts by Brussels to change behaviour in member states and companies.

"Women's capacities are not used in full," Jourová said. "The member states are losing several per cent of GDP, so this not only has a fairness angle, but also a pragmatic, economic angle."

The 'feeling' of equality is not the same as the reality as we see in the figures about gender pay gaps that only cover Europe. Globally the statistics are shameful. More than 50% of the population is being side-lined, ignored and discarded.

The value of women's contribution to life, work and the GDP is still highly overlooked, rejected and sometimes scorned.

How can you be yourself if you are seen as useless, worthless or unimportant?

How can you be genuine if you are told you have no talent, gifts, or abilities because you are female and originate from a certain race or religion?

How can you show your real genuine nature, your unique personality if you don't fit in?

How can you perform authentically when at the back of your mind and deep in your heart you feel judged?

How can you express yourself, reveal your creative talents, your imagination, your Einstein mind and flow of genius if you have negative and self-defeating labels sticking on you? These are the residues of restrictions, like the stigmas and stains of cultural and religious programming.

Blowing My Heart Out

One time I was playing in a popular and reputable reggae band. A famous Jamaican singer joined us to launch a new record and to feature three of his songs with our band. We had rehearsed the songs without him for over a week, and one evening he popped into the rehearsal studio to sing with us.

Everyone greeted him with the usual brotherly handshakes, hugs and exclamations, but for the life of him he did not know how to greet me. I was holding my saxophone and so I held out a hand, which he lightly touched with his fingers.

Now, the solo section for his three songs was traditionally taken by an alto sax, my instrument, but Mr. Honey Voice did not want a White Girl playing on his songs.

He went to talk it over with our bandleader, the drummer. I knew what was going on, not just from the volume of their voices but also the heavy sprinkling of dissing and cursing accompanied by mean glances from Mr. Honey Voice himself.

I have to give praise and thanks to my fellow Boys in the band for supporting me and appeasing him just enough to let me have a go. But I can tell you the pressure was on. I felt sick and shaky, doubting myself and dreading making any squeaky unprecedented sounds. How was this 'White Girl' going to handle the negative energy and rise above the low expectations of the singer man?

The trumpet player next to me said: "Go on G, you can do this, just be yourself!"

You see, I was asked to be myself, perform as myself! I was expected to step out from behind any stereotypical image of a tone-deaf White Girl, with no rhythm or sense of beat and perform authentically!

I had to gather up all my courage, confidence and competence in order to play eight short but sweet bars of sizzling and thrilling solo music.

As you may already guess, I had been in this situation a few times. But it doesn't make it any easier, because every snarl, mean comment or glare hurts and diminishes your confidence and courage. Doubting someone's ability to play, without even hearing them first is not a tactic used against men, but frequently against women.

How do you hold your own, stand strong and be authentic in these situations? How can you give your best performance when your capability has already been decided?

What do you have to do to swipe the prejudice from your mind, heart and soul and just be you? Because it is a huge part of finding your way to being genuine and authentic, and finding your true performing style.

When you overthrow all the negative pre-conclusions, discrimination and chauvinism, you can begin to reveal your personality with all its idiosyncratic features.

You will overcome the indoctrination and blackmail by recognizing that when you perform from the heart, mind and body, you are being you. Like wise, when you show and shine your mind, heart and body, you are performing your true self.

I did blow my heart out, squeaking a little, hitting a flat and a sharp sound here and there, but with my trumpet and trombone players at my side inserting their growls and whoops of support, I did a grand job. And, it got better as Mr Honey Voice got on with his job and I got on with mine.

Yes, I cannot deny the encouragement and support from my team pushed me forward. What would have happened without it, I don't know and I don't analyse it because a team means support and encouragement!

I gave my best and I performed from a desire to satisfy Mr. Honey Voice and myself – and I certainly didn't want to be replaced by a male Sax player.

Benefactors and Their Benefits

On numerous occasions people have commented about my performance as though it is an act, something **I do but am not!** I spent days, months and years rehearsing, developing my skills and learning how to express myself through an instrument. Does that mean it is a performance not an authentic demonstration of me? Is it not the bona fide me?

In my opinion, an authentic performance, or performing authentically, are one and the same thing. They are sisters, not broiling divas. They are compatible. They work and design together. They are the essence of you, the creative energy that you articulate in your own unique way.

Of course, performance can be interrupted and sabotaged. For example, when someone else redirects the work; a person who pushes you to behave in a way that is not you. Tina Turner was pushed and shoved around by the domineering Ike Turner. And, when she broke free from his chains, her performing style burst out in the most extraordinary explosive way. She found her authentic performance.

There are many examples in show business of women directed, bullied and bossed into showing up in a way that was not true to them, such as Mariah Carey or, famously, Ronnie Spector, the singer married to the most notorious Svengali of them all, Phil Spector. The fact remains that men still control much of the power - and the women - in the music industry.

In 2017, there were only eight women in top positions in the Billboard Power 100 list, revealing a hefty imbalance of powerful, wealthy and influential men at the top end of the music industry. Too many teenage female singers have been and continue to be under the control of the men at the top. Men control the studios, connections and negotiations and that means these young women do not have the opportunity to be themselves and to perform the way they want in the clothes and manner they want.

It is shocking to realise that 99% of producers are still male. In this unhealthy environment, young female talent has small or no chance of keeping a grip on creative, financial and personal control.

Women like Queen Latifah and Lady Gaga who are qualified to lead, don't have the powerful backing and connections to inspire, protect and launch young female talent into the music business. They lack the power and connections to sign contracts, mediate working hours and dress codes. In fact, they are unable to have any say or control in life style and the creative process.

The other alarming factor is that women lack sponsorship.

Economist Sylvia Ann Hewlett and her colleagues authored a study called "The Sponsor Effect: Breaking Through the Last Glass Ceiling" which states: '...women had a lack of sponsors – people who actually open doors for them as opposed to mentors who advise them on how to open the doors for themselves. Women have more mentors, but men have more sponsors, and sponsors are the people who wield the power to recommend you and really push you up to senior positions.'

I recollect endless times when bandleaders told me what to wear, how to stand, what to do before and after a show. I have had male members of bands tell me to go back to the dressing room and not mix with the audience after a show. I have also been threatened if I didn't offer sexual services to other better-known musicians as a favour to get our band in the limelight! And, yes, I have been forced out of bands for not obeying them.

That is when you know that your performance and authentic way of life is one and the same thing. Because when someone tries to mould you to his shape and design, you cannot be yourself, you cannot perform authentically. And this runs into any area of work, any area of life, where there are restrictions and control over your artistic expressions.

What is This Thing Called Authentic?

My experiences have taught me that being authentic is about letting go, refusing labels and not over-thinking. But wait; let's check this out in detail.

Being authentic

Is telling it how it really is. Saying '**No**, I don't wear thongs, drink cocktails, work for nothing, bend over backwards or believe everything you say.'

Being authentic

Is saying out loud what you want and then taking the relevant action. I want to be a singer, writer, photographer, financial advisor, pilot, footballer, physicist, director of companies, theatres and banks – and president too!

Being authentic

Is about your unique personality, showing it, rehearsing and practicing until you are proud. Making it work for you. Making errors, boo-boos and discoveries, and then making more mistakes and learning from them.

Being authentic

Is showing the best of you to the world and being recognised and rewarded for it too.

Being authentic

Is giving the best performance so you are heard, understood and believed.

Being authentic

It is stepping up and standing out. Using your courage, confidence and competence to fulfil your creative energies.

Being authentic

Is about releasing 'the rules from schools', written and spoken laws and brainwashing or cultural and religious programming. Saying, 'No, not for me!'

Being authentic

Is about learning, exploring, taking risks and opportunities in life. Developing skills to enrich your communication and your performance with the world.

Being authentic

Is saying, 'No, I don't want this, I've had enough.'

Being authentic

Is about defying and denying what doesn't gel for you.

Being authentic

Simply means that your expression is your genuine performance and nothing more or less.

CHAPTER TWO:
USING PERFORMANCE TO ESCAPE
THE CON BELT

The Power of Words

I believe that all of us are born with some gift, talent or special ability. It may be a skill with our hands, our voices, hearts, mind or feet, but we all possess some kind of special capability. And I believe we learn to bury that ability or conceal our talents early in life. We become trapped in a net. Some are self-made and several carry the Machiavellian stamp of society.

Then we meet our parents, the school, the college or the work place. Everything we have inside of us, all our natural genius flow is disturbed, agitated and too often re-designed. We are re-moulded and re-modelled by the modes and codes of the era we are born into: 'Don't use your left hand', 'You can't sing', 'Money is dirty', 'The rich are evil', 'You can be a teacher but not a leader' and so on.

We are familiar with the Jesuit motto:
"Give me a child until he is seven and I will give you the man."

Indoctrination of the young exists in all societies, most religions and, shamefully, in many warring nations. The training of boy soldiers in the DRC and Gaza is just one example of this early betrayal of children. Adults dedicate enormous amounts of time in the line of their duty to convince and implant what they believe to be true - unless they stop and question it all for themselves.

Adults have the power to enhance the dreams and desires of the young, or to shatter and destroy their natural abilities for life.

There is a tendency by adults, especially those in positions of power and privilege, to suck out any individual leaning – toward expressing flair, talent or natural genius - at an early age. Unless they seem some kind of personal gain from it.

This becomes clear when we see how for centuries, women had no formal opportunity to express their artistic talent as artists, musicians, sculptors, architects, surgeons and the like.

Mary Beard, in her extraordinary book *Women & Power*, reminds us from where many of today's insipid, misogynistic doctrines originated:

"When it comes to silencing women, Western culture has had thousands of years of practice."

She continues by referring to Homer's Odyssey, penned 3,000 years ago, when Telemachus, the son of Penelope, commands his mother to:

"...go back up into your quarters, and take up your own work, the loom and the distaff ... speech will be the business of men..."

And indeed, this attitude continues today, in parliamentary meetings, boardrooms and around many of the decision-making tables.

She refers to the 30-year-old *Punch* cartoon by Riana Duncan illustrating this imprinted 'deafness' in her infamous 'Miss Triggs' cartoon:

"That's an excellent suggestion, Miss Triggs. Perhaps one of the men here would like to make it."

The Official Cramping of Style

Many youngsters around the world find that their artistic potential is crushed as they are diverted to the Con Belt – the conveyer belt of work. A lifestyle that contains all the guidelines you will ever need to live an unfulfilling life. This is not just a Western phenomenon this is global.

The Pied Piper Syndrome that says, 'Follow me, I will show you a safe life that fits into the rules you have already learned and that have already been injected into you.'

In his epic book, *Sapiens, a Brief History of Mankind*, Yuval Noah Harari exposes the 'prison walls' created by Christianity, democracy and capitalism.

"You educate people thoroughly. From the moment they are born, you constantly remind them of the principals of the imagined order, which are incorporated into anything and everything. They are incorporated into fairy tales, dramas, paintings, songs, etiquette, political propaganda, architecture, recipes and fashions. For example, today people believe in equality, so it's fashionable for rich kids to wear jeans, which were originally working-class attire...the imagined order is woven into the tapestry of life."

Harari continues, "...every person is born into a pre-existing imagined order, and his or her desires are shaped from birth by its dominant myths."

And these 'dominant myths' affect the way we communicate, connect and develop in our society. If it is still considered a waste of time and money to educate girls because the belief, the myth is that they have no worth, no benefit, or no future, how can these girls find their genius, talent or contribution to the world? How can a girl perform to her full ability if she has no faith in herself?

Once again, Mary Beard agitates us with this question:
"How and why do the conventional definitions of 'power' (or for that matter of 'knowledge', 'expertise' and 'authority'), that we carry around in our heads exclude women?"

Cultural stereotypes are still in place and sabotage discreetly and blatantly the way women present themselves. Crushing and cramping your style and performance and re-directing you back onto the Con Belt. The methodology is 'behave yourself, do as you are told and don't veer off the road because you won't be heard, understood or believed.'

The Magic of the Alphabet

Words are powerful. They can make or break friendships, romance and business deals. They say words never hurt, but we know they can and they do hurt, because we can't always control our reaction to them.

From an early age, young minds are instilled with phrases that affect their self-esteem and impact their future, sometimes irrevocably.

I am sure you have heard these:

'Don't do that, that's bad, that's dirty, that's no good, stupid!'
'Oh, you dumb child, why are you doing that?'
'You'll never be any good!'
'You are such a disappointment!'
'Stop crying, you're a boy!'
'Don't play with trains, you're a girl!'

The list of damaging phrases is endless and we know how our children soak up and copy from adults around them. It all contributes to negative brainwashing and even worse, the negative language deviates us from following our dreams and desires.

Choose your words carefully - be diplomatic, don't shout, don't interrupt, be polite - is the guideline for us all, but the rejections and punishments, particularly for women who disobey this, are significant.

Words shape us. Words create our personal manifesto. Words inform us what we can do and what we cannot do. And negative words corrupt and pollute our ability to perform fully. We begin to play small, to hide, punish and reprimand ourselves. We fall by the wayside, we step into the mud and we stop, stall and stumble. We get caught up in nets.

Caught in the Net

Let's face it, we get caught up in things we don't always want to do. We become side-tracked or are enticed into doing something we are not 100% sure of – but we jump in anyway. Been there?

Have you ever been caught up in a net of deceit, corruption or bad vibes? Have you ever found yourself spinning downwards into a bad relationship, job or situation?

For many women getting caught up means to be trapped. Trapped in relationships, marriage, poverty, and jobs that offer little satisfaction and no way out.

We are dependent on fathers, brothers and uncles (if you have them in your life), or bosses, boyfriends and yes, pimps too. The fact is that so much of the power and privilege still remains in the hands of men.

Let me just recap on some recent laws passed in the UK. Just in case you were thinking it's all over and we have moved on.

It wasn't until 1975 that women could open a bank account in their own name.

Single women still couldn't apply for a loan or credit card in their own name without a signature from their father, even if they earned more, as recently as the mid-Seventies.
Working women were also refused mortgages in their own right in the Seventies, unless they could secure the signature of a male guarantor.

And in April 2018, *The Financial Times* reported:
'More than three out of four UK companies pay their male staff more than their female staff, and in nine out of 17 sectors in the economy, men earn 10 per cent or more on average than women. 90 per cent of women still work for companies that pay them less than male colleagues.'

This report came out just days away from the deadline for all employers in Britain with at least 250 staff to report the difference between what they pay their male and female employees.

How easily we forget the shameful discrimination against women that occurred less than 50 years ago and yet still continues today. And how hastily we dismiss the way it influences our choices and decisions in life today. Low pay and the lack of legal rights that leads to the undermining and detrimental effects of poverty, and stops a woman from expressing her true potential.

I know that I have fallen into several of those traps. In the music business, in theatre as well, I have been side-lined, paid less, given less credit. I became caught up in negative situations because I was hoping I could make it better, it was worth another go, another chance. After all, I am a woman and I am supposed to try, give in, and give it another go (all in one day). Be the strong one and forgive him, and all that jazz.

Performance Scores a Bad Press

Many words have changed their meaning over the last twenty–five years. Words we take for granted like truth and freedom, right and wrong and even yes and no.

Here's an example. In Old English, 'awe' referred to 'fear, terror or dread'. This later transformed into a solemn or reverential wonder, and 'awful' and 'awesome' were synonymous with awe-inspiring. Later, 'awful' took on a solely negative connotation, and the word found its modern-day usage to mean extremely bad. 'Awesome', meanwhile, evolved in the opposite way, probably in the mid-1900, and came to mean extremely good.

'Performance' is another word that has travelled a long road. The Merriam and Webster dictionary defines it as 'the execution of an action, something accomplished and the fulfilment of a claim, promise, or request.'

Fulfilment describes and interprets the definition of performance beautifully. It stands for achievement, accomplishment and contentment.

Unfortunately, there is a tendency to affiliate the word 'performance' with drama, theatre, something to do with the stage and acting. It suggests an act that someone does. Which is why it is often misinterpreted as 'inauthentic'.

Creating Your Own Traps

Getting caught up in any kind of net is life restricting, whether it is the performing industry, your badly paid job or a relationship. Women often trap themselves by making and then believing in a mountain of cleverly crafted excuses and rationalizations – both their own and other people's.

In their excellent book, *The Confidence Code*, Katty Kay and Claire Shipman interviewed Mike Thibault, a legendary coach for the WNBA (Women's National Netball Team). He spoke about training with women basketball players, including top professional players, the Mystics team, for whom he has been a coach:

"The propensity to dwell on failure and mistakes, and an inability to shut out the outside world, are in my mind the biggest psychological impediments for female players, and this directly affects performance and confidence on court."

Then, they interviewed Christine Lagarde, who runs the International Monetary Fund, who admitted to the authors that she "zealously-over prepares for everything.'"

It seems women head down the perfectionist road in trying to climb the ladder, break through the Glass Ceiling or Bamboo Floor or any other preventive device invented to hold women back. But as we know, perfectionism is a confidence killer and will most certainly supress and censor our performance abilities.

How can we avoid the traps and nets concocted by society and those we construct ourselves?

The net can be enticing for some women. The offer of money and a secure, better life is a real allure. How can you refuse a proposition of a new home, a safe place or an opportunity to work? Sometimes we just do not have the experience and/or the confidence to turn down the possibility of the dream life on display.

It is easy to make a judgement when someone else falls in a net. How accessible are phrases like, 'You should have known better', and the worst one, 'I told you so'? We remove ourselves from the suffering, shame and horror of trafficked girls by ignoring them, not employing them after they have escaped the net. We judge and condemn them for not fighting back, for giving in and allowing the torture to continue. We dismiss from our minds the evil lengths some men and women will go to make money and entrap women, girls and young boys.

Avoiding and refusing the magnetism of a human trap comes from experience and confidence.

Confidence can be learned but, like experience, it takes time, it takes support and collaboration and it takes some human understanding and love.

I believe that by understanding, recognising and acting on our true skills and our genuine abilities to perform authentically, we start to make conscious choices. These are the alternative choices that direct us to discover our full potential and to believe in ourselves and find that nourishing and flourishing life we want.

When we understand that the discipline of performance embraces every element of life, performance becomes the scissors that cuts the net, every time. Living life in a fulfilling way is about being an authentic performer, with courage, confidence and competence.

It is about escaping everyone else's rules by consciously making our own decisions about how we want to show up in life.

Don't let the 'the rules from schools' or the indoctrinations from ancient textbooks drown, dampen or suffocate your potential, your ability to perform. One of the most important steps we can take to reach our full potential and perform at our best, is to escape from the Con Belt system, ASAP.

CHAPTER THREE:
ALL YOU NEED NOW IS - THE CONFUSING WORLD OF ADVISORS, COACHES AND MENTORS

Some Very Straight Talk

We are guilty of turning the internet into the most popular Agony Aunt ever to sit behind a screen. If you have a question, a doubt or a fear, just tap it into your favourite 'magic formula' site and press Go! The answer, explanation, report, sign, feedback and solution will appear before your very eyes. Many will cost a whole pile of dollars, stamina and homework. Many will provide temporary comfort, enlightenment and more homework. And, many will keep you forking out till you become a clone of the person serving you.

Sounds cynical? Never happened to you? Let me introduce you to the online world of the Digital Nomad Coach Family. The people who will guarantee a six-figure fortune in 90 days, a following to shame Jesus and a bunch of neuroses that you have never heard of before but you will soon catch!

It seems a lot of people have lost their earthly connection to "Common Sense". Seldom taught at home, hardly ever at school and hard to find in a book. But one thing for sure, a lot of people are packaging it up in fancy language and celebrity names, and selling them like the sweetest hottest cakes going.

But as we know, common sense is neither common nor a sense. It seems we are being cajoled and guided back on to the Con Belt. The Conveyer Belt. It seems we have not accumulated enough competence, courage and confidence and therefore need re-training.

Have you been caught up in these perplexing nets? Do you feel that you have sat in front of enough coaches and mentors to pay for three luxury homes?

Do you think it is time to stand on your own two feet and use your own skills and talents to achieve what you want?

I think many of us have experienced coaching burnout. The addictive need to be trained just one more time, receive another certificate and see another testimonial posted on a successful person's web page.

We become obsessed with improving but never stop to credit our achievements and progress. We compare, and are unable to make decisions to Step Up & Stand Out in our own shoes.

For many women, this looks like the hardest skills to acquire and the most challenging of talents to accomplish. Perfectionism, prejudice and over-thinking stand in our way. And a world of miraculous gurus is waiting in line (and online) with their nets.

When women get caught up and over-focus on these time-consuming 'dis-eases', our behaviour changes, our performance suffers and we play small. We become the vulnerable bait. And our authenticity goes out the door like a vibrant mini tornado. How can we be authentic when we are copying someone else's step-by-step formula?

Yes, we need support and a team around us. We need learning and guidance and it is important to keep developing our skills. But let us not lose touch with our own incredible abilities; they are already part of our intrinsic design, our innate capacity. Let us recover our resources, resilience and unique genius. Let us start with encouraging ourselves.

My Meeting with a Messiah

I remember being lured into a coaching net with a woman who had decades of skills and many celebrity names to her credit. She was wise and experienced and liked to work with youngsters and those who did not doubt or question her. She wasn't used to questions. But question her I did.

Her method was to pull you down so far into your past, agony or insecurities, that you couldn't say 'no' to work with her. Because she had all the solutions.

Except I did say no – I didn't like the negative labelling; I frowned upon her critique and strongly disliked her direct hits on vulnerable topics. There was no encouragement and no positive outlook. She offered 'no way out'. You had to go through her hell to find yourself! Pain, suffering and plenty of crying guaranteed.

I stood up to her and told her my opinion about this kind of negative training. A few supported me privately but most were scared of her. A verbal exchange like glistening sharp swords ensued. From my side, it wasn't about winning but about making a point, not to lord it over those in need, those who are hurt or damaged from the pains of yesteryear. I wanted to progress and improve, not dwell on the past.

The personal development guru with the broad smile poked and prodded at me, searching for my weakness, prying for a place to use me as an example of her skills! Her game was to push me as close to the door as possible so I would open it and leave, and leave a neat pile of bank notes too. I represented trouble, rebellion and mutiny. I didn't cry or breakdown and that offended her. I should have reported her to the Board of Gurus – but hey, there isn't one!

Be vulnerable they say, reveal your heart, but who is there to help you rise up after the Guru has pushed you into that hole of hell? Only the sheep that follow will receive redemption, praise and prizes. Sounds like another one of those Messiah stories to me.

Beware of the Guru with the halo, the ones willing to steal your power and fire. Before you part with your energy and money, look around, ask and check out the bigger picture.

A mentor is someone who sees more talent and ability within you than you see in yourself, and helps bring it out of you.
Bob Proctor, Motivational Speaker and Entrepreneur

Knowledge is as Good as having Freedom

Many a phrase has been quoted to summarise the benefits of gaining knowledge.

Knowledge will bring you the opportunity to make a difference.
Claire Fagin, American nurse, educator, academic, and consultant.

Knowledge is power but has little value unless it can be easily accessed and put into practice.
Melany Gallant, Content Manager at Talent Management Solutions Company and blogger.

And I would add that knowledge is something to be shared.

Education and our access to greater learning are essential to progress and improvement. We search for a person who can guide us, open our imagination and encourage us to greater endeavours. I have invested time, energy and money in becoming more professional, broadening my knowledge and advancing my performance.

I have found excellent teachers, instructors and partners in crime to work with. People who supported me, showed me new avenues and doors and gave me enough pushes, kicks and suggestions of the right and bright kind to move on up.

I am sure if you remember back to a teacher who gave you that extra attention, that thrust and burst of optimism and confidence to go forth and do your thing, you are smiling now.

Unfortunately, there are still many who do not have the right or the access to education. Especially for women and girls, there remain huge challenges, set-backs and a negative attitude towards their education. This pessimism still exists today. Less overt and subtler but the prejudices and chauvinism remain, institutionalised and embedded in the DNA of women and men.

There are numerous campaigns promoting the rights of girls, offering access and opportunities to train and learn in positive and conducive environments. But it is not global; it is not available to all. Perhaps this lack of education, this shortage of role models and absence of women at the decision-making table affects our confidence?

How much of this lack of representation affects our attitude to being more courageous and confident and attaining greater competence has been researched and studied extensively. There is no doubt that the suppression of the education of girls and women has had dire consequences worldwide.

What the Papers Say

The Confidence Code by Katty Kay and Claire Shipman outlines this dilemma comprehensively.

In their interview with Christine Lagarde, Head of the IMF, and Angela Merkel, the German Chancellor, they uncover the immense preparation that women at the 'top' undergo in order to be seen as good enough, competent and confident.

"We have talked about it," Madame Lagarde confided, referring to her conversation with Madame Merkel. "We have discovered that we both have the same habit. When we work on a particular matter, we will work the file inside, outside, sideways, backwards, historically, genetically and geographically. We want to be completely on top of everything and we want to understand it all and we don't want to be fooled by anyone else."

Here are two highly educated and powerful women of the Western world doubting their experience and expertise, and admitting it. We know that women are notorious in over-thinking, over-analysing and over-labeling in the preparation for any performance they undertake.

They have turned the preoccupation of being as perfect as possible into an Olympic sport, as Kay and Shipman repeat in their scientifically researched book:

"The shortage of female confidence is more than just a collection of high-octane anecdotes...it is increasingly well quantified and documented."

What is most interesting is when they ask the same question about confidence in men, they report that men are just not as bothered about what others think:

"They don't examine those doubts in such excruciating detail, and they certainly don't let those doubts stop them as often as women do."

They discover that women hesitate at key moments and hold back because:

"They aren't often sure what scorecard will be used to judge behaviour. And they are afraid to get it wrong."

Sounds like a lot of self-sabotage going on. How is it that we women keep driving down the lack of confidence highway? Why are we so self-critical, especially when we know that it leads nowhere and has damaging consequences?

I have learned that competence, courage and confidence can be learned. They are skills to grow, develop and learn throughout your life. And, when you put them all together you have a powerful mix, an authentic performance and a strategy to succeed.

Competence gives courage, courage leads to confidence and confidence shows you how to communicate. Win plus win-win and a bonus. Once you have understood and started consciously implementing them into your life, they work together and in many combinations. Individually, they lead you onto the next step; they guide you to show up as an authentic performer in your life.

So remember, as Kay and Shipman so succinctly phrase it:

"Perfectionism – on our growing list of confidence killers."

Let's Go Bungee Jumping!

Some people immediately associate bravery with acts of fearlessness and extraordinary displays of courage of a physical kind. I personally would never go zip lining, bungee jumping or skydiving. But I will do many things that would scare the cave divers, rally drivers and cage fighters.

To each comes a unique version of courage and bravery. But what is courage? How do we measure or recognise it? Is it different for women and men? Is a man brave when he steps in to protect or save lives, as in a fireman, lifeguard or policeman?

And when is a woman considered brave? Is being a single mother being brave, or coming forward after sexual harassment or rape? It seems our indices for bravery have gender differences. Perhaps this is why we just don't admit or perceive female courage.

Bravery is the capacity to perform properly even when scared half to death.

Omar N. Bradley, Chairman of the Joint Chiefs of Staff & US Military Policy Maker.

So, is courage about facing up to your fears? Is it about being physically strong and resistant to pain? Is it about resilience and being consistent even when things are tough? Is courage about knowing your limits, showing patience and wisdom?

Be brave. Take risks. Nothing can substitute experience.
Paulo Coelho, Author

Mel Robbins tells us that:

"Courage is a birth-right. It is inside each and every one of us."

That suggests it is just a matter of bringing it out and encouraging acts of courage at an early age. But we know that courage is not just a physical act. It is also about **speaking up, stepping out and standing up for yourself**.

Just Do It!

Nothing builds confidence like taking action.

It is noticeable that when girls and women enter into sports and other physical training as in dance and music, courage and confidence take on another meaning. Is it the competitive influences and the desire to be brilliant that builds the courage and confidence? Is it the acquisition of competence in your field and your profession that strengthens your resolve to be excellent, professional in your performance?

There are still barriers for girls and women to excel in the physical arts. The struggle to be recognised as sporting heroines continues. Open any newspaper or TV sports programme and it is a lucky day when a female sporting event is mentioned.

In the last few decades women's participation in sport has been significant. But disparities remain and are prevalent globally. It is the lack of funding, sponsorship and spectator support that are the guilty culprits. Once again, it is about seeing female role models participating at all levels, receiving media coverage and financial backing that will encourage more girls and women to entertain and perform, just as men have had the privilege to perform whenever and however they want.

Whether we take up netball, volleyball or any other ball, the same opportunities and investments must be present. Developing physical abilities for personal or professional benefit is about recognition of your skills, the way you approach confidence and the building of your own personal courage file.

And these are the very skills that define your performance on any stage, in front of any person.

Women have been bullied to sit still for too long. Our physical capabilities are disapproved of and discredited. Even in childbirth, we are subjected to lying on our backs. It is time to experience the full physical presence of women. And that includes the incredible skills of pole dancing too! Women have been dancing backwards on high heels and juggling a lot of balls. It is high time for some financial support and rewards. Time is up to give professional status and opportunities for girls and women wanting to take up physical activities for fun, for life and professionally. And these physical skills have immense results on our competence, courage and confidence.

Step Up & Stand Out

I started this chapter expressing my dislike and distrust for the phony world of transformational coaching; for the self-proclaimed Gurus who seek to trick and cajole the vulnerable into poor replicas and clones. And who hide behind a fake mask affirming authenticity and success. They have created a convincing vocabulary, a stream of empty phrases that actually encourage more mental unrest.

Yet, I have also stated the enormous benefits of having that Einstein influence in your life. A teacher or mentor with knowledge, imagination and your interests at heart. People who will expand your competence, courage and confidence and make it work for you.

I do believe that there are excellent individuals and organizations available to advance, amplify and awaken our natural abilities, so we can believe in ourselves, make decisions and express our talents with competence, courage and confidence.

It is important to remember that everything we do in life is about selling. We sell our time, energy and skills.

We sell our backs and minds. We can call it exchange or barter or give and take. But it is all about swapping something you have for something she or he has.

We spend our lives selling, showing and sharing what we have in exchange for more time, money and love. Meanwhile, on the way, we meet a thousand and one challenges. And for us to overcome them we most certainly will need competence, courage and confidence.

It starts with believing that you have greater reserves inside you than you think. But it is not just about strength; it requires flexibility, openness and learning to make decisions that you act upon.

It is also about questioning and challenging anything and everything that goes against your grain. Knowing when to take advice and information on board and when to refuse it. It means being honest and brave enough to say no when things feel false or unreal for you.

- Trust your instincts.
- Believe in your common sense.
- Exercise your decision muscles.

CHAPTER FOUR: HAVING A PROFESSIONAL MINDSET AND ALL THAT JAZZ

The Panto Syndrome

What is the difference between an amateur and a professional? Does money or habit come to mind when you first think of the distinguishing lines between being professional or amateur? Is it about attitude and recognition? Is it all down to how famous or infamous you are? Is it a combination of all these things and perhaps a little extra dose of *'je ne sais quoi?'*

Has the line between being professional and amateur blurred a little? And how does it affect your ability to perform? Do you hold back as an amateur? Or give more as a professional? And at what point do you become professional?

When we are encouraged to 'give our best and show them what we are made of', we usually make every effort to do so. But if you are told you are just an amateur or you are not professional those phrases can cramp your style. The negative implications of being amateur or not yet professional enough can hinder and damage your spirit and therefore your behaviour – and ultimately, your performance.

The suggestion behind these judgments is that you are not good enough. You will always be second-rate, you are not quite making the mark and when are you going to get a real job?

In the world of music, theatre, fine arts, spoken word, writing and dance, you are often accused of being amateur if you don't receive money for your work. It is a sticking point for many. If you are not making money you are not professional. But surely there is more to it than that?

The Tower Theatre in London is an amateur theatre company, which puts on over 20 productions every year.

And it is just one of the 2,500 amateur dramatic companies in the UK which stage more than 30,000 productions a year. Does this mean it is a frivolous kind of amusement? Hinting of a patronizing or condescending prejudice that it is less? Is there still a snobbish attitude towards amateur entertainment?

From my experience, professionalism is a mindset usually accompanied by financial rewards for excellent and valuable work performed. It is an attitude, a way of life and the manner in which you express your creative skills. And it shows in your performance.

There is also the expertise, experience and excellence that go into the making of a professional person. It is a blend of consistent dedication that involves repetition, practice, time and learning.

Having a professional mindset is crucial to giving a top performance. Because every time you give the best of yourself, you perform authentically.

The 'Fake It Till You Make It' Chicanery

I am all for the 'go for it now' attitude and 'action speaks louder than words' approach. But the 'fake it till you make it' scenario is such a contradiction of words. Why do you have to fake it? Why are you trying to fake it? If you want to be authentic how can you then fake it?

The big question that rattles around my head is **how** can you fake it? If you want to start a business, go bungee jumping, become a singer, writer or baker, how can you fake it? Surely you have to go through some learning process first? Acquire some practice, guidance and rehearsal?

To become professional in our life and work, we go through a learning experience. We may learn from others, do the hands-on method or go through some other form of instruction, training or drilling.

The human desire to be the best we can, to perform authentically and offer a first-rate version cannot include a 'fake it style', a 'pretend it until you get there' expressway.

If you try and fake your performance, guarantee you will be spotted. Whether it is a fake presentation, blog post or orgasm. You will be discovered.

If we take pride in our work, we feel satisfaction, self-confidence and even self-respect - and then we know we are performing authentically.

So, let's inject some chutzpa into our bones, or take a spoonful or two of sugar but forget the 'fake it till you make it' boulevard - it just is not real.

One Step at a Time

So, if faking it isn't the answer, what is? Somehow we have to bridge the gap between being a beginner and an accomplished professional. And in that gap, that learning phase where experience is accumulated, many types of blurry lines appear.

Doubts pop up all the time. Will I ever make it? What happens if I fail? How can I please everyone? In the beginning, we don't always understand what is needed to attain a professional mindset.

When I first started out in music, I made a quite a few booboos. Like everyone, I didn't want to make mistakes; I wanted to be brilliant from the beginning.

In those early days of blowing the saxophone, I have to confess, I sounded like a dying sea cow. To dampen the ugly vibration and give it more body, I would run scales facing in towards an open wardrobe full of clothes. It blunted the squeaks and rasps and softened the acoustics but it couldn't cover up the mistakes.

I learned over a period of years that mistakes are the best teaching tool that there is. No one plays the piano, paints a picture, writes a book, gives a speech, or acts in a play without considerable work, rehearsal and more learning. It is not about focusing and fixating at what the successful have. Check out what they did to get there.

In 1992, at the age of 57, Annie Proulx published her first book, *Postcards* and then, a year, later the award-winning book, *The Shipping News*.

It takes years to become an overnight success.

Education is about gaining knowledge, training the mind to think, and then utilizing that information to develop your talents and skills. During our lifetime we take onboard new information, we train and exercise new things in order to develop our abilities and create that nourishing and flourishing life.

I believe that along the road of learning, we meet muses, mentors and fellow team players. These are the people in our life who will share their wisdom, and show or encourage us to go forward. There's nothing like learning from those who have been there before you.

The King and I

Two or three times a week, I would take myself over to Ray's home and we would stand facing each other with our alto saxophones almost touching, blowing out sheets of sound.

It was the best hands-on, private tuition a budding player could ask for. Ray A. is a highly talented, multi-instrumentalist. He plays drums, piano, guitar, congas and saxophone. He has knowledge and a couple of decades of working as a musician. In my eyes he is a top professional.

He'd blow a phrase, stop and wait for me to repeat it. I'd go over it as many times as I needed until I got it.

Then he would play the next 4 bars and I would repeat until I had them under my fingers and in my head.

They were mostly 16 bar jazz standards, but not the usual easy ones like *Summer Time*. Ray challenged me with complex music from Thelonious Monk, Coleman Hawkins and Charlie Parker. I had to sharpen my ears to hear every note played and then find it on my instrument and play it back - soulfully.

I learned those tunes without seeing a single written note and when I had them fluently, Ray would play a counterpoint melody over the top. He had a magical, sweet sound full of fire, energy, soul and inspiration. My job was to keep the beat and play the melody. How easy it is to write those words!

There were enough times when Ray would stop, look down at my feet and ask,

"Tap out that rhythm for me again?"

I knew instantly I had lost it.

"That is quite some rhythm, how do you do it?" he'd add, giving me a perplexed look.

I could deal with his sarcasm because he was also patient. After a few moments, he began tapping his feet and counted me in. Off I went once more to play the melody. He would wait to let me get a tight hold on it and then blow another extraordinary song just 50 cm from my face. When we got it right, or rather when I could keep the beat, play the tune and not crumble when he played some extraordinary counterpoint notes, it was beautiful. It was pure sound, harmonic excellence.

I was so excited to have this opportunity to have Ray as my mentor and teacher. But when I told my friends, they would say,

"What does he want from you?"

"Do you pay him?"
"Are you in his band?"
"Is he famous? He must be rich!"

When I responded,
"Nothing – no – no and no," for each of those questions, the response was disappointment and comments about it just being a hobby. And then, "Oh, amateurs having fun."

Damaging words to hear as a budding player, learning the craft from a genius musician unable to make a living but, nevertheless, a professional. Or is he just an imposter? Am I just doing my hobby because I am not working in a band that's making loads of money?

It is confusing because it does matter. It matters to our morale and self-confidence. Being a professional means a certain amount of visible success doesn't it? So, if being professional is about how others see you, then the outward signs, the financial rewards and how you are perceived matter a lot.

My mentor Ray from my point of view is a professional musician. But he is not headlining, living in a palace or appearing on TV tonight. Does it blur the lines and cause confusion? It feels like we have created an enormous amount of stress and pressure around those two labels, professional and amateur.

The Learning Never Stops

In the arts, in languages and in life the learning never stops.
I am studying life every day and as soon as I feel I have learned something, I soon find there is more to learn. It is as if the more I know the less I know!

As a child, the messages I heard at home were, 'Keep trying', 'Don't give up', 'Try another way' and 'Say it differently'. Behind it all was the idea that what you really wanted, what you needed, wasn't clear enough. So, say it again, and say it using different words.

There is always a way, another path, another adventure or doorway to discover. Keep learning because there is always something new to learn that will enhance your strengths and build on your weaknesses. After all, these are the elements that make a professional.

Attaining your knowledge and expertise are the first steps, but at what point do you become professional? When you get the certificate, the award or golden star? Is there a turning point from amateur to professional? Is it tangible?

I know for myself, if someone says or even insists I am amateur because I am not successfully earning money and my kudos ratings are low, it is just a judgment and an assumption on their part. As a professional with a professional mindset, I shake off such comments. They have no relevance to me – my interests and my concern lie in my work, my performance.

A Professional Woman

So, is it any different for a woman to achieve the professional badge of honour? Does a woman have to do more, dress to kill, provide extra services, and look amazing day and night or perhaps, all of it?

I know many women who say you can never know and never win. It seems that in order for a woman to be considered professional, she has to jump through more hoops of fire than the men. With all the barriers and tricky credentials required of women, how does it affect our ability to be ourselves and perform to our best? If we are constantly asked to behave in a certain way that goes against our grain but not that of the company, business or stage, how can we remain authentic?

I know I have changed my appearance and attitude to fit in, to get the job to gain the audition. I am sure you have too? But then what? How do we cope living and working in a disguise that doesn't fit in with our values?

"I witnessed so much appalling behaviour by male musicians, writers and other music biz types that I often felt as if I had wandered into the gents by mistake." Penny Anderson, writer, journalist and former A&R scout in the music business.

Carla Marie Williams, who has written lyrics for artists including Beyoncé, Britney Spears, Craig David and Girls Aloud, says, "The music industry is still a 'boys' club' where women are not given enough opportunities to develop. We need more investment by record labels and publishers to involve women at a younger age to bridge the gender gap."

It seems the rules are tougher for women in the professional world. Women are expected to perform better, reach higher standards before they get into the professional club. Yet, until more women sit around the decision-making tables, the amateur hat will be thrown at us.

The lines are blurred between the professional and amateur. Some make it over the line and some don't. Many are learning that money isn't the only criteria, perhaps even more so for a woman.

For a short time, I assisted a friend of mine who worked as a music tutor at the London Film School in Covent Garden. Most of the young filmmakers were young men; the training ground for future documentaries and entertainment movies still created, written and directed by men.

I stepped in to write bursts of music for the short films the students made. Many didn't want music because they felt it would take away something from their artistic style or it would cover up the real meaning of their story. How naïve they were! The music and film industry are firm bedfellows; they rely heavily on each other to secure hefty dollars at the box office and beyond.

These privileged students would often question my expertise and competence.

"Is she professional?" they would ask the male expert tutor, whom they considered professional. Assuming I was low in rank, not qualified or professional.

"We are not working with her if she is a student."

Did I have to invent some kind of professional persona to convince these students of film that my work, my contribution to their films was professional? Did I have to play some inauthentic character to assure them they were working together with a talented musician, writer and arranger? Did I need to have a penis to qualify?

For an artist, writer, actor, sculptor, painter, dancer, or any budding entrepreneur, there are numerous situations when the discussion about your professional or amateur status arises. It seems we are still judging and assuming others in order to satisfy some lack in ourselves.

For me, the most pertinent measuring tool is behaviour, attitude, presence, style and performance. I believe you have to find a formula, a method, or a course of actions to acquire that professional mindset. Here are mine:

- Disarm your critics but listen to feedback from mentors and muses you know and trust.

- Never stop learning your craft. Watch, read and observe the professionals you admire and respect.

- Say yes to opportunities. Take risks and learn from your mistakes.

Don't let others take control or discredit your performance; create your own professional mindset and show them what you are made of.

I tend to agree with Cecil Castle:
"Professionalism is a frame of mind, not a pay check."

CHAPTER FIVE:
THE FOUR FABULOUS SISTERS

It's a Family Affair

Imagine growing up with four sisters like Consistent, Persistent, Resistant and Insistent and having them support you throughout your life! Sounds crazy but I tell you with a little imagination you could conjure up four good friends or four team members, or perhaps call them your biz buddies.

At your side you would have **Consistent**, encouraging you to continue and go forward, to be regular in your actions. She is the sister (or biz buddy) who is dependable, steady and constant, and shows you how to progress in your endeavours.

Her twin sister, **Persistent**, would then stand by you and show you how to endure, be relentless in your pursuits, sometimes resolute, and always determined.

Your third support, **Resistant**, is defiant, bold and daring, showing you how to be tenacious in achieving your dreams, beliefs and goals.

And lastly, **Insistent**, a support and a sister who is assertive and compelling, she is decisive and confident and shows you how to never give up on those dreams, beliefs and goals.

What a family, can you imagine? What an enviable line up of allies!

What if we had this kind of backup during our years of education?

How we would excel in life, make smart decisions and choices, with these savvy sisters guiding us.

There are many times when I could have used the guidance and counsel of those four. During my volatile teenage years when I felt insecure at every corner, I would have lapped up their wisdom.

Those Tedious 'Rules From Schools'

At school, I learnt about 1066 and how to make a sponge cake. In my opinion, this information was totally irrelevant. And had nothing to do with the complex world around me at the time.

My creative talents were frowned upon and I was considered to have poor concentration. My school reports stated I was lazy and unable to sit still. And this had nothing to do with the school curriculum? Nothing to do with the way teachers opened up the top of our heads and poured in dates of kings winning or losing battles.

Yes, I remember Henry VIII: he was the one who *consistently* and *persistently* found ways to marry a new young woman and murder the last one. He was *insistent* about changing the laws and fighting the Church. He *resisted* all kinds of pressure from his peers and advisers – and if they interfered too much, he changed the law again and found enough faults to banish, or murder, anyone who got in his way. And the lesson is...?

I remember being asked to read Henry James, Charles Dickens and a whole host of male authors who wrote about the lives of men and often excluded women or treated them as ignorant and useless chattels.

In an article from *The Guardian* newspaper dated Saturday 23rd February 2019, Ian Jack reveals the appalling and misogynistic behaviour of one of the British education system's literary giants, Charles Dickens. He was a man who gave to the poor and wrote about their suffering in Victorian England. But behind closed doors, he led a double life.

"Domestic tyranny was a fact of Victorian life: men who were saintly in public could behave very cruelly behind their front doors.... Dickens' worldwide reputation as a compassionate moralist – the enemy of humbug and suffering – continued to flourish untainted by the facts of his private life."

A collection of 98 recently discovered letters reveals that Dickens' wife, Catherine, gave birth to 10 children (let's remember that rape in marriage was common) and yet managed to outlive him by 8 years. She 'tolerated' his long-term affair with the young actress Ellen Ternan, keeping it a secret from his adoring public. But the worst was to come, as Dickens tried to lock Catherine up in a mental asylum, a common practise at the time for bored husbands. In fact, a woman could be imprisoned in a mental asylum if she was suffering from melancholia, imbecility and mania.

These were the characters that filled the heads of girls and boys at school. These were the heroes of children, the Jekyll and Hydes of real life. This was the indoctrination that men could do anything and get away with it. And this was just the tip of the misogynistic iceberg. This was school!

How I secretly longed for my own personal Fabulous Sisters, to reassure me that there was more to the world than this, that there were many thousands of healthy, caring and appreciative boys and men out there, not wanting to subdue me or lock me up.

Fame After Failure

There are numerous examples of women and men starting out to create a business or become professional and failing. Failure, they say, is a normal and even healthy occurrence. And there is always a choice. By adopting the qualities of Persistence and her three siblings, you have the opportunity to get on, move on up and start over.

I love the story of Jean Nidetch, a housewife from New York who was overweight. She loved sweet things and was unable to drop any weight although she tried many diets. In 1961, at the age of 38 and weighing 97 kg or 15 stone, she decided to invent something herself. It was a simple plan: to create a healthy diet and do lots of talking with women with the same problem. The idea was to be accountable to each other and share healthy recipes.

Within two years and having lost more than 30 kg, or 5 stone, Jean Nidetch began her global business, Weight Watchers.

There are other inspiring stories where pushing through failure gave motivation to persist. J.K. Rowling had manuscripts rejected by 12 main publishers. Oprah Winfrey was fired on one of her first TV shows and called *unfit for television*! Walt Disney was fired by his editor at the *Kansas City Star* newspaper because he *lacked imagination and had no creative ideas!*

Jean, J.K., Oprah and Walt used their Four Fabulous Sisters to reach their goals. They decided to open the doors to opportunity.

We also have stories from women and men in our own lives. From family, friends and neighbours, who performed acts of determination that captured our attention. The stories of those who never gave up and continued until they reached their goals.

I think we can all remember the energy we have when we want and desire something enough to make changes and take action. Something inside us stirs and we push through previous barriers, try new tactics or pursue another road.

We double our efforts because our intention is to get that job, gain the scholarship, win the race, and land that book deal or prestigious talk. Our determination is at a high level; we are functioning in 'I will get this' mode.

Pushing through the obstacles and setbacks with the help of our Four Fabulous Sisters, or Biz Buddies (or you can call them your Best Brothers). They are the force behind your failures and successes.

My Mother Told Me

When I was growing up, my mother told me, "If you can't get in the front door, try the back. If the back door is closed try a window. And if that is locked up, go down the chimney. And if that entrance is blocked, build a 'frikken' tunnel!"

It was all about persistence and being consistent and insistent and being resistant to negative feedback and mini failures. It taught me to go for it again and again. It showed me how to ask a question, to ask for guidance and/or advice. It taught me to not give up, to find a solution and not get bogged down in the problem.

We know that behind each person who pushed through was the energy and passion to persist and succeed. It is the driving force to crash through barriers, obstacles and failures. This spirit, this strength, derives from the Four Fabulous Sisters: Persistence, Consistence, Resistance and Insistence. And we all have access to them.

I believe there is something more to it than just passion and determination. I believe that your personality plays a big part in this story and even more, your performance skills.

Practice Makes You Proud

If you think about an occasion when you wanted to get in through a door, any door that was important to you, how did you prepare yourself? Did you fuss over your clothes and hair? Did you rehearse a few lines? Did you perhaps check it out in the mirror?

Maybe you even ran it by a friend or wrote it out? How did you prepare for that next open door, the next opportunity on your path to achievement?

When we set out to impress, to take up a new offer, to speak in public, write a book that has been brewing inside of us for decades, or start that business plan, how do we prepare ourselves? Most of us begin with drumming up the confidence and courage to take the first step.

Yet many of us find it hard to know how to come across as confident, professional and knowledgeable. It is as if we don't know how to behave, to show and shine our personality – to perform. We don't know what role to take or how to act. It is as if our innate ability to perform when we communicate is deadened, numbed, filled with inhibition or shame.

And now we even have a name for a person who has a mountain of skills and talents but is not confident enough to drive forwards in their business. We call it 'imposter syndrome'.

I have found that in life if you want to make an impression, connect and engage, you either have to prepare or you already have prepared. And that means you are experienced and have done it before. During that preparation, you create a role, an act you decide upon, and you design the behaviour you will display. You are preparing for your performance. Recognizing and utilizing your innate performance skills involves the talent and co-operation of your Four Fabulous Sisters. Once we acknowledge and accept them into our world, embrace them and start to take action with them, changes will manifest.

Those of us who are aware that we have a real team of support in those Four Fabulous Sisters, know we are not alone, know that we can dig that tunnel, climb in through the roof or build a door.

It is not about jumping on the merry-go-round of life, dictated by others, but stepping off that Con Belt and creating the life you want.

The Sirens are Calling

For me, those Four Fabulous Sisters are essential to my overall performances in life. I call upon them, arouse them and sometimes cry for them to assist me in my endeavours, struggles and adventures. It is about training my ears to listen out for them and I admit, there are times when I am deaf to their support. Sometimes I get bogged down with emotions and feelings that don't serve me.

Then, like sirens, I hear them calling out to me, to be persistent and consistent. They say, be strong, resistant and insistent with my actions. They push me to stick up for myself and to perform with courage. And most importantly, those Four Fab Sisters, encourage me to show to the world the real me with all the sugar and spice that I carry.

We all have times in our lives when our resistance is low, when our powers to be consistent and persist with our ideas, dreams and goals feels futile, even near the end. If only we could see over the rainbow and jump aboard the fast train to success. If only we could conjure up a touch more energy to insist upon the next move.

Like everything we do in life, the awareness that they are there for us is the simple answer. To recognise and believe you can go through with it, persevere, finish the job, improve, reach the flag, put down the last full stop, whatever it is you want to accomplish, remember you have those strengths inside you – those Four Fabulous Sisters.

Dialogue with the Sisters

Georgia   = G
Chatty Monkey   = CM
Consistent   = C
Persistent   = P
Resistant   = R
Insistent   = I

CM: Georgia, do you know you aren't getting much engagement these days - have you noticed?

People are moving away from you. Look at the stats!
You are just not saying anything hot anymore.

G: Go away!

CM: That's not a good attitude to have; I can see why your followers are bored.

C: Ignore him – you are consistent and you offer variety, that's what counts.

G: You think so?

C: Oh yes, even through your troubles and travels you are present.

P: Yes, and let me add that your tenacity is noticeable and people respect your determination.

CM: No one can see those things - they are just big, empty words.

R: Don't listen to him Georgia, you are gutsy and dependable – great qualities.

G: Yeah, you're right, thanks Sis.

CM: But with all the millions of people out there doing the same as you – I mean picture it. They are just more engaging, more intense, more valuable than you – I mean no one can see you anymore.

I: Just remember Georgia, your work is compelling, decisive and confident, people admire those skills.

C&P (speaking together): Shall we grab that Chatty Monkey and take him for a long walk?

R&I (speaking together): Yeah, we are up for that too.

G: Thanks Sis, that's right - a long walk!

CHAPTER SIX:
HOW TO GET YOUR MOJO BACK

Love in the Winter Sun

On New Year's Eve of 1991/2, the stirring in my bones was telling me to make some changes in my life once more. I am open to change and often long for it, create it and conjure it up. My philosophy is that everything is temporary and it starts with life itself. Change can be scary but I look for the excitement too; and so for me, change is scary and exciting.

It is a great way to approach your daily performances, being open and ready to change. Whether you find it scary or exciting or a combination of both as I do – tuning in to the stirrings in your bones can lead to new opportunities.

As leadership expert Robin Sharma says:

Change is hard at first, messy in the middle and gorgeous at the end.

I was restless with the way things were going in my musical career. Glass ceilings, or those made from concrete or bamboo were cramping my style, giving me a malaise of frustration and a sour taste in my soul. I needed a change.

In January 1992, I was asked to join a friend of mine out in Tel Aviv, Israel. Winter in the sun, how could I refuse? It was an escape, an adventure and an opportunity to revise and review my options in life and the first steps towards change. I thought and then decided. I packed a case for a short stay and did not take my instrument with me. That's right, I left my saxophone at home.

Now, those were the days when I never travelled without it, even though I was relentlessly pulled aside, called up and detained for carrying something that looked like a small machine gun.

It didn't matter what I was wearing, smart or casual, but a woman with a Sax was still a rare event. The questions thrown at me started with these:

"Why are you carrying a case that looks like gun?"
And the second question when I was forced to open the case:

"Can you really play that?"
The third regular question was:
"Are you carrying drugs in there?"

I had a whole list of ready-made answers, from,

"I keep my nappies in there."
to
"No guns, only hand grenades."

And sometimes I would say that the case was full of sexy underwear. None of those answers helped the situation when in front of border guards or police officers. But I was a rebel with many causes.

Three Wise Men

I took the flight out to Tel Aviv without my saxophone, my head and heart open to some new inspiration. As it turned out it was a journey of adventures, surprises and romance. It was also the first step to bringing writing back into my life in a whole new and fascinating way.

The person I was going to stay with (who is no longer alive and therefore I will not say anything good or bad about) had changed his plans due to a sudden, serious illness. He had experienced a stroke. As a result, his speech was slurred, his energy was low and he didn't want me to be there.

"We are going to Jerusalem," he said, as I got into the waiting car after I cleared security.

"You won't like it, you shouldn't have come but now you are here, you can stay with me."

Now that was an invitation I couldn't refuse.

Jerusalem is 1000 metres above sea level and it can snow in winter. It is also a city full of religion, conflicting religious history and religious anger. Already, I too was wishing I hadn't come.

When we arrived at the apartment we discovered there was no bed or sofa bed in the spare room. My host shrugged his shoulders and said,

"I have to sleep now, make yourself at home."

He went to his room and closed the door.

I stayed seven weeks in Jerusalem even though on that first day, seven minutes was feeling like too much! I am resourceful, resilient and of course, know how to call on my Four Fabulous Sisters to show me a way through any nightmare. But I was regretting coming out here.

One by one, the friends of my host came by to help and hinder me. I sat down with his three best friends, an orthodox Jew, a Greek orthodox Christian and an Iraqi Jew. They helped to provide the essentials – clothes, food and a bed. All three showed me the best parts of the city according to their point of view and I was grateful to have their company. Walking alone as a woman in a new environment always requires vigilance. When you add religious and cultural differences the need for vigilance and caution increases. Walking around the city in the daytime, I soon experienced the eye daggers and nasty verbal insults spat at me, by religious men, dressed in their uniforms of hypocrisy. They shouted at me,

"Whore of Babylon!"

According to Wikipedia, the Whore of Babylon, or Babylon the Great, is a symbolic female figure and also place of evil mentioned in the Bible's Book of Revelation.

Her full title is given as 'Babylon the Great, the Mother of Prostitutes and Abominations of the Earth.'

So, the logic must run that a woman roaming the streets, unaccompanied, is a threat and a danger to men and therefore must be veiled and hooded. Laugh or curse, this is still society's rules for many women around the world. Imagine how that stifles their skills and talents to perform every day.

I deeply dislike divisions related to history that no one can agree upon. I strongly oppose religions that de-humanise women and girls, and position men and boys on superior pedestals. I was not feeling at home.

Search and ye Shall Find

Within days of arriving, my fingers got itchy. My lack of musical expression was giving me withdrawal symptoms. And on top of it all, the religious energy in the city was getting under my skin. I felt stifled.

What do you do when you get the itchy fingers feeling? What do you do when you feel your style is being cramped, your performance held back? When you feel you have more to give and the bigger picture, your bigger picture is just around the corner?

Do you go out and search for something else? Do you encourage yourself to go out and find something? Do you say, never give up, like I did? I do believe in finding solutions rather than harping on the problems.

One bright, cold and sunny morning, five days after I arrived, I stepped out of the apartment and walked around the nearby streets, searching for some inspiration, something to distract me and occupy my itchy fingers. In a positive mood, I decided this was the right city to discover a miracle.

I went with the breeze; I followed my nose and let the explorative energy of the day take the lead. I saw a doorway that caught my attention. Caribbean flags floated above and sweet soul music entered my ears. This was a miracle!

The café was dark but I could easily make out simple wooden tables and chairs on either side. At the back I saw an open door letting in sunlight. Then, I saw a piano and made a beeline towards it like it was my long-lost love. The poor thing creaked and squeaked, it was illogically flat and sharp at the same time!

The owner of the café approached me and offered me a drink and a snack on the house.

"To make up for your huge disappointment with the piano," he explained with an irresistible smile shining on his face.

We drank coffee, ate olives and toasted almonds and could not take our eyes off each other.

You see, nothing stays the same; everything changes and moves, grows or dies.

During my seven weeks in Jerusalem, I found love.

I saw almond trees in bloom; I listened to the smooth Sax of Joshua Redman at the café of my new beau. I was caressed and praised, my woes and worries were ironed out and almost every night I saw the moon.

I started to write. Words came flowing out of me and on to any scrap of paper I could find. My new sweetheart bought me a writing book. I scribbled continuously. The love he showered upon me came out as beautiful poems. Talk about the gossamer wings and moonlight on our naked skin - it was all there.

Georgia On My Mind

But on my mind was my life in London and my Saxophone. I began to think about the musical opportunities waiting for me. Love in the winter sun is a beautiful experience but I knew, we both knew that it was only a short affair. I was ready to climb back up and go get me some exciting new musical projects. Love had filled my confidence vessels and I was ready to return like any Jedi.

My second night home, I went down to my favourite club of the day, Ronnie Scott's in Soho. The guys at the door told me it wasn't the usual; there was no music, just some guy on stage talking.

I figured that I was closer to a stage than my bed, so I went in. There was an electric atmosphere with the audience on the edge of their seats focused towards a dark stage with one spotlight aimed down on the head of a young man wearing a kind of Zorro cloak. It was black on the outside and red on the inside, and he kept flashing it about. He had a thick Glaswegian accent, lilting, deep and yet clear. He paused and gazed down at his audience with wild, dark eyes. There was fire and rebellion within him in massive proportions. He strode about with grand movements, a proud walk, his head held up high.

Twenty minutes later came the finale. He stood facing the front of the stage; his left arm went out at his side and he snapped his fingers.

A tall man came on, dressed like a waiter, with a large silver tray in his white-gloved hands. He handed it to the main man and walked out backwards, bowing slightly.

Larry MacLauchlan did not move or blink, the tray steadily balanced in his outstretched hand. He paused a moment longer, bought the tray to the front of his eyes, now holding it with both hands.

He inhaled. You could see his chest rise up and then exhale forcefully, aggressively, all over the white powder contents of the silver tray.

It flew everywhere, not just to the first rows of the audience, but to the sides too, as Larry inhaled and exhaled, and spat his breath and the white powder all over his excited followers.

There was laughter and screams, and roars and shouts of 'Me, over here!' and 'More, more!', and 'Over here too!'

Larry MacLauchlan was triumphant and he moved back bowing at each step, nodding his thank you, as the rapture in the audience got louder.

Was it icing sugar, white flour, ground up aspirin or cheap cocaine? No one cared. He had ensnared them, he had captivated them and they wanted more. And I too wanted this. His words, the story I cannot remember, only his extraordinary Performance. I was caught in his flying white energy.

This was the inspiration I had been searching for. It was the magical combination of words and drama. My imagination was soaring. I walked across the road to the Italian café and sat sipping café with the late-night crowd sharing what I had seen, discussing the ingredients of the tray and was Larry MacLauchlan real?

Mixing with Your Crew

This is why I believe it is so important to view and support fellow Performers, Artists, Musicians, Playwrights, Poets, Dancers Authors, Sculptors, Videographers - anyone who pronounces, articulates or voices their creative and imaginative talents through some form of expression.

We find inspiration and energy from entering their worlds. We discover role models and teams when we mix and mingle with them, the like-minded. We develop confidence and courage to accomplish and achieve our own adventures and projects.

We learn about performance. We learn how to integrate those skills into our unique work, our original designs, businesses or books. We learn to understand that everything we do depends on, relies upon, and is deeply rooted in our performance skills.

The next time you go out to listen, view or be entertained by an event or activity, notice how you react to it. Be aware how it influences you there and then, or later. Recognise what you take away from it all. See how it inspires you to do something else, something different in your life.

There are occasions - for example after seeing a live band - when I am so energised, I begin to write something new. Or I want to talk about it and share that special energy with a friend or colleague. You know that contagious energy we receive when we are open to absorb and feel something new in our lives? Inspiration comes from human connection.

Whatever it is for you - a ballet, a boxing match, a book launch, a new exhibition of paintings, a play or pantomime, a rock, reggae or hip-hop band - it doesn't matter what lifts your spirits and gets into your soul. It is more about that magical connection you experience from being part of someone else's performance.

Notice how you become energised and motivated to do or try something new or different after experiencing a dynamic performance. Take this opportunity to explore the performances that feed your creativity and imagination. Even if you don't find a creaky piano, love, or white powder, I guarantee you'll find something.

CHAPTER SEVEN: CARVING OUT YOUR PLACE IN A WORLD FULL OF WORDS

How to Develop Courage, Chutzpa and Balls

I recently watched an interview with the former Australian PM, Julia Gillard, in which she admits she has been an active feminist since her university days. She tells us of her surprise and disappointment at the flagrant, misogynistic and sexist vitriol that she experienced while she ran that vast country. PM Gillard regularly made speeches, spoke in public and took part in TV interviews and was often verbally abused in the most crass and vulgar manner.

It left me with a bad taste in my mouth to hear that a woman in a prominent public position with great power at her fingertips experienced and continues to be exposed to such unabashed masculine abuse.

Yet at the same time, it gave me a strange feeling of solidarity and comfort. The feeling of solidarity obviously fills that lonely vessel of not being on your own, not feeling like a mad woman imagining it all, because so many women and men think it has all gone away. This is the twenty-first century, there is equality for all.

Julia Gillard has the strength and smart angle of using wisdom and diplomacy to disperse the malevolence (male–violence). Her cool appearance and intelligent presence informs us how to handle the venom, how to diffuse, dissolve and dislodge the hostility and rise on up as women and Go For It.

And there are numerous examples of women in the news, on screen, paper, or radio experiencing nasty, insulting and disgusting verbal attacks. Just ask around.

I too wanted to speak about the injustices and the unfairness that women face.

I wanted to rant and rave about our skills and talents and show the world there are so many variations of women. We are not just red heads, blondes and brunettes.

I knew it would take courage, chutzpa and balls to stand up on stage and speak about the topics that mattered to me: those taboo situations that affected me and so many women and girls. Above all, I had to follow my gut feeling, my artistic instinct, the truth bursting inside me that said, 'Go Out There and Perform it Now!'

Talkative Music

After seeing that almost magical performance by Larry McLaughlin with his tray of white powder, an idea to reinvent myself began to germinate– again. An image of me performing with words, music and a touch of drama started to flourish in my imagination. It was the beginning of my journey as a Performance Poet, as a musical Spoken Word Artist. And I called it Talkative Music.

I started writing with a passion and determination that could only be described as wildly ambitious. It was bold and provocative, controversial and rebellious. I read and devoured articles, prose and poems from famous and infamous writers. I read translations from Hungarian and Israeli poets that stirred my soul and itched my boots. I became mischievous and devilish in my writing and couldn't wait to jump on the stage and deliver.

First, I hit on as many Performance Poetry clubs as possible, trying out my material. I went from hip venues in Hammersmith, like the Riverside Studios, to the numerous dingy rooms located at the back of pubs, North and South side of the River Thames in London.

It was exhilarating and hectic but much of my work was not received well.

They said it was too provocative, confrontational, too sexy, too much sex, too frightening, too unreal, too real, too in your face, too rude, not real poetry and yet somehow funny. That sounded like a good summary of me, and many other women I know!

Strange and familiar things were happening on that Spoken Word scene back then in the early nineties. It was competitive and cocky, and yes, that means there were a lot of Boys on the scene. It seemed that the audience was comprised of three main categories. A third were budding poets, another third were aspiring poets and the last group believed they were poets.

The scene was intimate, the talent predictable and the clubs run by bossy guys and I was slowly making enemies out of all of them. I had to insist my name was down to perform because the diversions and sabotage going on was incredible and ran like this:

"Oh, sorry, I didn't see your name there."

"It's not here, oh, did you write it down yourself?"

"Here it is, well, I can't read it at all. Did you write it?"

And the best was: 'I called your name but you didn't answer!"

The attitude of the guys towards female poets was hostile. But if you were smiling, pretty, young and ready to listen to all their talk, they liked you. I was not ready to play the 'yes game' and the 'I will shut up while you talk all night' game or the one which was all about 'praising, analysing and more praising their poems' game.

Surely there were other ways to tackle this hostility other than being aggressive or massaging egos? Was it that only Boys could talk about injustice, war or global destruction? There were several guys performing great pieces about topical and current events with fire, drama and passion. But us Girls had to be demure, flowery and nice?

And again, I turned to my Four Fabulous Sisters for strength and courage.

Pamphlets and Booklets, Alive Alive Oh

I had to get my shovel out again and dig another inroad, gain some ground and build my reputation. I had some hot poems, topical, radical and relevant. I would print up the words and create a simple pamphlet, a collection of ten poems wrapped up neatly with a card cover. I had a great photo on the front with a title and my name. It was like a business card.

I carried my pamphlets on stage with me for every performance and even when they didn't applaud, or just murmured approval, I sold every copy I had with me. On stage, they didn't approve but back stage they came a-running, and paid two pounds a shot for my little pamphlet.

I became known for my snappy booklets and lively musical performances.

Some of my pieces had rhymes, and I could recite them like a rap which, let's face it, not many White Girls were doing back in the early nineties. Soon enough, all the guys had pamphlets and it became an 'I'll swap mine for yours' scene.

For a short time, I had diverted the hostility by creating something they wanted – the booklets. But soon enough, the novelty wore off and with everyone flashing their pamphlets around, my popularity waned. Maybe that's why you haven't heard of me!

Mary Beard explains: "The more I have looked into the old patterns – it doesn't much matter what line you take as a woman, if you venture into traditional male territory, the abuse comes anyway. It is not *what* you say that prompts it, it's simply the fact that you are saying it."

Let's face it, women have been denied a public speaking voice for thousands of years. Ridiculed and condemned to shut-up. Just study the Greeks and Romans and then glance at Homer and Shakespeare, or Leo Tolstoy, Charles Dickens, or Ernest Hemmingway to witness the mass evidence of male supremacy and hatred towards women.

Slipping and Sliding

I was slipping and sliding on that glass ceiling again. Why was it so hard to get up on a stage and talk? Why were there so many boys and men jumping up and speaking and sharing their opinions? I had to look into the disparity between the number of women and men on this Spoken Word scene.

Back then, even performing at some back-street pub for free you had to stick your elbows out to get a spot. And often I was the only female performing. The first ever female poet laureate was Carol Ann Duffy, appointed in 2009 after 341 years of the honour being awarded to males.

Nowadays, we have the Slambassadors, Apples & Snakes and some truly inspiring names, like Jawdance and Tongue Fu. The spoken word scene has grown and exploded and become part of spoken word education programs. The Poetry Society encourages thirteen-to-eighteen-year-olds to take part in poetry competitions and many girls rule that roost.

However, Lucy Crompton-Reid, now ex. Director of Apples and Snakes, points out:

"More women are taking to the stage at open-mic nights as headline acts, and also in poetry slams. Yet it would be fair to say that, currently, there are probably more male spoken word artists working at a particular level in terms of their public profile; it feels like we are at a point of real change, with more female poets bringing their work to a wider audience."

Female Spoken Word artists are rocking their poetry on video, stage and page and talking about important, heartfelt subjects. What do we have to do to get the world, more men to listen to our words?

In journalism, another writing profession, a report in 2016 showed shameful results:

"The British journalism industry is 94% white, 86% university-educated and 55% male, according to a damning survey of 700 news professionals conducted by City University London. ...City's research indicates that women are paid significantly less than their male counterparts. Nearly 50% of female journalists earn £2,400 or less a month compared with just a third of men."

In January 2018, Carrie Gracie, a senior journalist employed by the BBC for 30 years, revealed publicly that her male counterparts were being paid 50% more for the same work. She stepped down from her job after a highly publicised dispute between her and the BBC over the disparity of her pay.

She remarked about the BBC:

"It is like talking to a dodgy car dealer: they know they have a faulty vehicle and they are trying to sell it to you. You need to be signalling to them that you are not going to stand for that."

And so, still today, inequality of pay between women and men continues even in established institutions like the BBC. How does this situation encourage you to do your best? What strengths and courage do you need to enter any professional business if you are constantly facing this Two-Rule Approach?

I'll Do It My Way

After nine full weeks of crawling from one place to another, sometimes three venues in one night, I felt I had done my groundwork. I wanted more and I wanted to work with music.

I was also missing the team spirit, the collaborative creative energy of working with musicians.

I hunted around for a musical companion, someone who could play rhythm and leave me to talk, rap, and express the words on top. I kissed a lot of frogs, and then I found a bass player who loved my lyrics, and could hit those strings and create rhythm, rhyme and music in a way that complemented my words like a dream. It was going to be sensational.

A new magical show was evolving. I was excited and focused, and felt that now I had found a combination of expression that fulfilled my musical ideas and gift for language.

As George Bernard Shaw says:

"Life isn't about finding yourself, it is about creating yourself."

And this is why performance is so critical to living a fulfilling life.

Hostess with the Mostess

I decided that the only way to do this was my way. I negotiated a club night at a small venue in Chelsea, with the admirable assistance of my handsome and charming bass player.

We would headline with a twenty-to-thirty-minute set and then open up the stage. I wanted to mix things up and so offered the space to other budding talent. Most nights, it included one singer, a guitarist or keyboard player, a comedian, an actor to do a monologue or mime and, of course, the poets performing words from their pamphlets, hearts and heads.

It was becoming known as a cabaret venue and, every week, surprise acts would show up. The club had a capacity for about twenty-five guests, and the stage couldn't hold more than four or five people. By week four, we had to turn the performers away.

We had enormous challenges, mostly with the owner who had the bar upstairs. I couldn't understand him as our thirsty crowd spent money in his cramped bar. I think he had the greedy eye, or maybe a bit of professional jealousy.

Nevertheless, The Talkative Music sessions continued to blossom. We had many laughs but barely broke even. It lasted six months.

I didn't realise how much unexplored talent there was in London and how many untalented people wanted to climb on stage. There were great lessons in diplomacy to learn. I had the task of deciding whom to accept on stage and whom to turn away. One poor act a night was tolerable, and the audience always let you know if you were hitting the mark or not. Everyone was so close to the stage you could hear every word.

The Boys loved heckling; it was a popular pastime all over the poetry and comedy scene and often ugly. I hated it and soon found my tactics and ruses to get them out or to shut them up.

For me, as the Hostess with the Mostess, I had to learn to be quick with my responses but smart and gentle with the content.

The other big challenge was getting more women to step up and perform. I encouraged women to come and jump up on stage. I searched around the other clubs supporting and asking them to come and perform at the Talkative Music club. Lack of experience, confidence and guts were the reasons they gave for not taking the opportunity to try out their material. Sometimes it was hard to understand how even shy fellows would get up and perform but the gals seemed to be over-thinking, over-analysing and under-estimating themselves.

So many gave up, some couldn't handle the competitive energy, the testosterone vibe, or simply said, 'My poetry is more for the page.' Many of the women stepped away from the hustle and aggressive atmosphere of the Spoken Word scene. It was tough and predictable; it was the usual ceilings of glass faced by women in the Arts and beyond.

Never Say Never

I began to look at the American Slam Poetry scene with both eyes wide open. All over the East and West coast of the USA, the cities were brimming with fast, competitive Slam contests. Now, I am not particularly into individual contest but the team slams got me thrilled.

I thought to wet my feet on this side of the Atlantic and bounced on the first event down in Bristol. In November 1996, Bristol hosted one of the early British Slams. It was going to be an individual spoken word show, where each person had three minutes and no more to render their finest piece.

I had never entered a Slam and laughed my head off when I saw scorecards scattered around the audience seats. It was like in the Olympics. There was an 8.5 card, a 9.2 and a 7.8, and then I saw the 3s and 4s. On top of it all, there were some of the London crew, the Boys Brigade, The Pushy Bosses, the guys who really did not like me, standing in line to talk me off the stage! I tell you that night there was not only a lot of white powder flying around but also fat droplets of angry testosterone.

But I won the Slam Contest with a poem titled 'No'. A subtle and tongue-in-cheek piece about the power and the pleasure of a little word like 'No'. It was a memorable night for me, yes. I had gained some kudos as a writer and performer, but there was a delicious satisfaction about the words of the poem. The sound of the word 'No' echoing in the building like a defiant reverberation of the dynamic effect the word has for women and men.

From that dynamite night in Bristol, I found the team that would take me out to the East Coast Poetry Slam in the summer of 1997, in the USA. They were like-minded poets from the spoken and written arena, who encouraged, guided and showed me the new avenues. And so began another phase as a travelling Spoken Word artist, a team player, a Slam competitor on the American stage.

I learnt so much from taking the chances and challenges and being brave enough to re-invent myself. I wanted to be heard, understood and believed. I wanted to be taken seriously as a writer, performer and entertainer. I didn't want to hide and deny my feminine energy, my female mannerisms and cover up my sexuality to fit in with a standard or a norm that wasn't me.

I found my way, the 'never say never' way. Once you step into your unique gifts, talents or skills, really believe in them and take action with them, opportunities come. And if they don't come, you create them: you dig that tunnel and take action in another way. It is about focusing on solutions, not living in problems.

Our energy for life, our talent to express and perform to our zenith is part of looking after numero uno –**You**. You are significant, you have something important to say, and it's vital to keep going, even when the world tells you otherwise.

CHAPTER EIGHT:
THE 'TWICE AS GOOD' SCENARIO

Cultural Programming

Whatever women do, they must do twice as well as men
to be thought half as good. Luckily, this is not difficult.
Charlotte Whitton, Canadian feminist and mayor of Ottawa.

In a world where women are seen as the talkers, it still surprises me that there are so few women on the Spoken Word scene. Women love communicating through words, it is our best and worst communication tool.

The linguistic theorist Jennifer Coates has called it 'the androcentric rule', whereby the linguistic behaviour of men is seen as normal, and the linguistic behaviour of women is seen as deviating from that norm.

And herein lies the ominous controversy. Women's voices have been curbed, silenced and denied for centuries. The opinions, ideas and inventions of women have had little or no importance – let alone recognition – for thousands of years.

Women are censored, suppressed and muted. We have been gagged, restricted and subdued. Yet, we have the reputation of being chatty, gossipy, gabby and nagging. How can we be both?

Is it to do with being culturally programmed to listen to men? Are we accustomed to receive the words of men as authoritative, knowledgeable and truthful?

Women working in the corporate arena are still complaining about being talked over, having their ideas ignored only to be 'invented' five minutes later by a man. They call it 'mansplaining' and it is widespread.

Sadly, women are complicit in this inherited, subversive behaviour.

We don't speak up, we laugh when the men are funny and remain silent when a woman has a bright idea. And why do we do this? Is it a fear of losing our jobs, our positions? Is it because we don't want to be seen supporting the enemy, the underdog, other women?

In the Show Biz World, there has always been a pressure to prove to your bandleader, director, producer or any of those in the role of employing you, that you are the best and inevitable choice. When you apply, audition or persuade the boss to consider you – you know you have to give the performance of your life. You have to show them that you are not only good enough but also the best thing to make their show, event or programme fly high with bells and awards on top.

All those wanting to get that job, that role, or that position, face a challenge. And, when we want a new position, whether it is on stage, on camera or behind a desk, we make a special effort. We practice, revise and rehearse our words. We design a script, a pitch or a sentence to impress. We prepare to perform our hearts out in order to not be refused or rejected. We put together the best compilation of ourselves to make us memorable, irresistible and the one they want. We design a unique performance.

That is the playing field and we also know it has never been an even one. The criteria for employing women and men can be summed up in one polite word: unfair.

In 1935, Noel Coward wrote a song titled, *'Don't put your daughter on the stage Mrs. Worthington.'*

His lyrics make it clear that Mrs Worthington's daughter was not pretty enough, clearly too large, and didn't have the right teeth. A girl like her would never succeed and should not apply. Was the song banned? Was there any outrage over these sexist, biased lyrics? No, not all.

The Fear of Blacklisting

In the world of theatre, the prejudice is thicker than you can imagine. Julia Pascal, a British playwright and theatre director who owns a theatre company called Pascal Theatre Company, states clearly that:

"The exclusion of women from equal employment at all levels flouts both civil and human rights. The theatre is a serious, international political platform. It is a parliament of the arts, a form of soft power and a cultural territory as important as any physical land mass. With this abnegation of female flair, audiences are robbed of the full human story. These audiences are 65% female.

There has never been a female artistic director of the National Theatre or Royal Shakespeare Company. Sir Nicholas Hytner, artistic director of the National Theatre for 12 years, until March 2015, never directed a play by a woman during that time. Women may occasionally appear as actors, directors and playwrights, but the English stage is devoted to worshipping male narratives."

Where are the histories of our mothers, sisters and grandmothers?

I have seen this disparity so often and I have witnessed outrageous harassment, insults and degradation of female actors, producers and even directors. Surely we have moved on from Shakespeare's time when women were not even allowed upon a stage or had their tongue cut out by the rapist in order to shut her up? (As in the case of Lavinia in Titus Andronicus.)

Julia Pascal continues,

"There are structural reasons for marginalization. Drama schools educate female graduates to expect lower employment levels than their male peers. The actors' union, Equity, the majority of whose members are female, rejects calls for equal representation.

Most important of all is the position of ACE (the Arts Council of England). This unelected quango crushes female ambition by boxing women into a category called diversity. This term reduces women – the majority of the population – to a minority. This promulgates the lie that females are diverse and males are mainstream. Orwellian double-talk maintains male dominance."

Right on Julia Pascal! Women are not a 'diverse' group! No one would dare say men were a diverse group either. Diversity exists within each of those genders, but not specifically in one.

Hopping Mad

When I was 20 years old, a friend of mine enticed me out to Munich. He had a lovely apartment and was set up with a market stall selling Indian jewellery where he had met loads of fun people who were doing street theatre and making money. I didn't hesitate. I took a coach out there, two days and nights bumping on an old bus for something like twenty pounds sterling.

The first month was fantastic meeting, greeting and facing many new challenges, with language and lifestyle. It was exciting. But no one made any money.

I had a friend who had a friend whose father worked in a bank.

"Meet him," they said, "You might get a job or something."

I wasn't keen, I mean walking into a bank was a rare event for me, but I did.

Hans was not just the manager but also the head of the branch. He was smart and elegant in his appearance and offered his hand across the desk as I entered his large office. We chatted easily, or rather I did, telling him about the market stall and the street theatre and that neither made money. He had a hard time smiling and crossed his legs several times with impatience waiting for me to stop.

Finally, he said:

"I can offer you some secretarial work, typing and filing that kind of thing."

"I can't type," I said.

"What? A woman who can't type is like a woman with one leg!"

I swear to you, I got up and started to hop around the room.

After what seemed a very long moment in time, he began to laugh. And, of course, I did too.

We went for lunch; it wasn't a smart restaurant as I was dressed in some long hippy type dress and he in his designer business suit. I had a good meal and we laughed a lot or, rather, I made him laugh.

Chalk and cheese, fish on a bicycle, it really was two different worlds. From time to time he would suggest a job I could try.

"You could do a waitress job, a cleaning job or how about a nanny job!" he would say with excitement in his voice. He was solving the problem of a wayward girl and taming the shrew at the same time.

I had showed and shared with him my skills and talents as an imaginative and creative person coupled with my sense of humour. But he couldn't see any potential in me. He was unable to offer me an introduction to anything else but serving, cleaning, or nursing children and men.

Once again, even though I had put on my best and most charming performance to Hans, I was just a girl.

The Facts We Hate to See

Have things changed? Is it easier to get on in life without stripping off, lying down and grinning and bearing it?

Are we still being judged as 'just a girl?'

It seems if you look at it one way, amazing progress has been made. Yet, if you turn to the other side, the truth of the matter is shocking.

Data for the US and the UK indicate that just over 4% of airline pilots are women. This number is growing, but very slowly. According to the International Society of Women Airline Pilots, the big three US airlines have the highest number of women pilots and the Indian LCC IndiGo has the highest proportion (13.9%). However, consistent global data on women airline pilots does not exist.

According to the British Law Society 2017, figures showed that women are still under-represented in the judiciary with only 890 court judges (28%) and 806 tribunal judges (45%) being female. In the high court, 21 out of 97 judges (22%) were female, and in the court of appeal nine out of 38 judges (24%) were female. Fourteen of the 66 deputy high court judges (22%) were women.

The number of women CEOs at Fortune 500 companies fell by 25% in 2018. At the Harvard School of Public Health, there are still huge challenges facing women taking on leadership roles.

Pay gaps and gender inequality stretch right across all professions. The struggle to be considered and then accepted continues.

Girl Behaving Badly

I remember as a teenager going for an interview at a University. It was back in the day, way back last century and I was asked why I didn't want to teach children. It was their first question to me and it stopped my brain. I was studying English Literature and Sociology and I wanted to learn about drama and art.

"I don't want to teach children," I said, with too much defiance in my voice.

The three-piece panel of judges whispered to each other and cast their judgment upon me.

"You should teach nursery children," said one.

"It's a natural vocation for a girl," said another.

"Why don't you want to teach? Is there a problem?" said the third man.

I did not impress them with my manner, my opinions or my attitude. I failed completely in my performance. I did not live up to their expectations, or their idea of how a woman should perform.

I am sure you know what that means? When you walk away without the job or the position and believe you have not given them what they wanted. In this case (which was repeated at three other Universities, shame on them!), I had the same judgmental questions thrown at me.

Why wasn't I interested in teaching children? Imagine how disappointed I was that I couldn't get a place at a University because I didn't want to teach children? Imagine if I really wanted to teach children but somehow didn't fit into the narrow category the three-piece panel expected?

Whatever answer I offered they, the panels of mostly men but some women too, had reached their conclusions which clearly defined me as:

a) Not normal
b) Unfit
c) Unnatural

Even back then there was a dire shortage of male teachers. And in 2016 the Department of Education in the UK published statistics for the numbers of teachers and, in total, only 26% were men.

Where are the male role models for boys? Perhaps men and boys don't think there is a need? I find that logic illogical, don't you? And over the next decades those infuriating and insulting questions may have toned down but the results are the same. There are not enough men in teaching.

Old News

The 'twice as good to be considered as half as good' scenario has been around for many centuries. Women of all races, ages, backgrounds and skills have been on the receiving end of this anomaly and it goes on – and on.

It could be the 'in your face' method, as in the outcry of a US politician recently:

"Why are there so many educated women in the room?"

And as recently as 2019, a female barrister, who has young children, was told, by a male judge: "You should really think about whether the bar is right for you," after she raised childcare issues when he wanted to sit late.

And then there is the seemingly subtler yet more subversive version:

"Oh, you have a degree."

Even though there are and continue to be significant signs of progress in many areas of life, women and girls still have to prove themselves twice as much. And I know from personal experience how this affects my psyche, my attitude, my drive and my ambition to succeed in life.

Being turned down, rejected and/or pushed back down the ladder is a blow to anyone's determination. When we get knock-backs, we are told it is normal and healthy, we are informed it makes us stronger and it is good for us to comprehend that you can't always get what you want.

I think that is just brainwashing us with negative beliefs, and an attempt to drum these into our souls. But what makes it double tough and treble hard to swallow is that just because I have a pair of tits and not a pair of swinging balls, my ability, skills and performance are judged on different criteria. And it is a whole list of judgments based on ancient, unproved and unscientific hearsay.

The stereotyping of gender, race, religion and class runs deep in our societies. But gender stereotyping is at a global epidemic level. Even though progress has been made on so many levels, the gaps in pay, in human rights, and in control over our bodies and minds is still in the hands and laws of the masculine-led societies.

Archaic, Antiquated and Antediluvian

There remain 12 countries where women struggle to place their vote. Most are held back by religious wishes of Islamic men. For example, in Pakistan, women can vote - but there are no gender-segregated poll stations, so they cannot vote.

In Saudi Arabia, Qatar, Oman and Afghanistan, women gained the right to vote but are prevented from leaving their homes without male permission, or are dictated to vote a certain way by the male guardian. (There is now an app available in Saudi Arabia, sold by Amazon and Google for a male guardian of any age to follow and control the movement of a woman).

But top of the list is the Vatican City, where women do not have the right to vote. Women are unable to hold any executive or legislative positions in Vatican City elections - whereas men can become cardinals.

The twice as good to be seen as half as good dis-ease continues. It is subtle and it is blatant and it hurts and it angers. It makes you want to rebel or recoil; it has a degrading effect on women and men. This is inequality, double standards and, at its worst, misogyny - and it damages men too. And what about the next generation?

We need role models to encourage us, to show us how to develop a sense of 'yes, I can do it too.' When you see someone just like you doing something you would love to do, it inspires you to try it. It is simple human nature. When you see your girlfriends signing up to be a flight pilot, a chef or a political candidate, it must inspire you. And, most of all it encourages you to put on your best face, your best boots and lipstick, and get out there and perform.

We are like chimpanzees, like babies and we learn from copying and imitating. We have within us a natural genius to express this – if we are encouraged and are given the chance. And, if we are allowed to show and share our own unique abilities to perform, we can succeed with our wildest dreams.

Twice as good to be seen as half or not at all, or sometimes if you don't bend the right way, has to be exposed. It has to be driven out. The taboo must be cracked so we can flourish and perform to our full abilities. We must talk about it with our friends, our children, old and young. We must share our experiences and let people know what is going on, and make it clear that it is not just a rare event.

Time to Step Up & Stand Out!

CHAPTER NINE:
PUTTING ON THE GLITZ

The Pros and Cons of Looking Like a Woman.

*We have no template for what a powerful woman looks like,
except that she looks rather like a man.*

Mary Beard

Every time we step out of our homes we pay some kind of attention to our appearance. We go through a series of rituals to prepare ourselves for the outside world depending on where we are going and whom we may be meeting.

If we are shopping we choose practical garb. If we are going to do sports we climb into our stretchy outfits. If it is an important meeting, like a job interview, a possible promotion or new business adventure, we probably follow a dress code. We are always preparing and arranging our image so we can go out there and perform.

We want that job, we need that promotion and we want to impress the guys at the gym. Whatever the occasion, we dress to kill. We dress to impress and we dress to show who we are. We add a little perfume, scarf, deodorant, an earring or necklace to show we care about ourselves. We are conscious about how we want to be seen and/or received.

We humans have been doing this for centuries, following fashion or rebelling against it. The fashion industry impacts on us daily and many women and men indulge in the fluctuating styles in one way or another. Whether we are aware or not, whether we like it or not, how we appear is commented upon, critiqued and weighed up all the time.

How we react to the comments and opinions of others affects our performance, either for the better or the worse. If you are a follower of fashion, a rebel or eccentric or believe you couldn't care less, how you present yourself to the world is noticed.

What you wear, how you appear, speak, use gestures and mannerisms, are all part of your daily performance skills.

I remember watching a speech given by Meryl Streep. She came on stage wearing a strong patterned black and white jacket. She stood behind a lectern and began. Within 30 seconds she stopped and looked up at the audience because she had noticed they were distracted, chatting and whispering.

She moved forward to the front of the stage, leaning in and asking: 'It's my jacket isn't it?'

She didn't wait for an answer but removed it and stepped out to the left, then the right modelling said jacket for the audience to view.

When she returned to the centre stage she said,

"Now you have seen the jacket, the lining, the whole design, let's get down to the talking!"

The audience settled down, laughing, shifting a little, some still discussing the jacket. But Meryl had taken the jacket out of the equation of distractions. Now you could say, why did she choose such a loud outfit, or why this or why that, but comments would have been made about her dress choice, no matter what.

And for women, this is a common, every day and night experience. Yes, they also make the comments and the judgments; they have grown up learning this negative tactic, dishing it out without thinking, because everyone does it. Because it helps you define who you are and helps you fit.

Not Fitting In

For about six months I was working with a reggae band, mostly touring the Midlands of England but based in London.

I remember nothing of Birmingham, Nottingham, Worcester, Wolverhampton or Telford. It was during the winter months and we would start our drive out of the city around three or four pm when it was already dark. Our return home to London was always at six am, once again in the dark.

The band consisted of a drummer, bassist, guitarist, keyboard player, singer, and trombone, tenor sax, trumpet and myself, on alto. We often had a driver who doubled up as roadie. Those were the hazy days of traveling with nine men in a van. Does that sound exciting or terrifying to you? Does it suggest adventure and some sexual encounters? I can assure you, my book about Me and Nine Men in a Van will be written and published soon!

The Boys were gregarious with each other, noisy and loud. They talked about sport, food and their instruments. They sang and hummed riffs from songs and our repertoire and only argued about politics. At first, I was keen to add to the banter and have a laugh with the Boys. But often they just bellowed over the top of me.

Most of the time, they acted as if I wasn't in the van. They hardly ever asked if I needed to stop, wanted a drink or needed something. I wasn't shy about asking for what I wanted, but I was self-sufficient and carried with me what I needed. When I pulled out a piece of fruit, I'd shrug my shoulders to say, 'can't share this – sorry.' I guess they called me mean or greedy, but I didn't listen.

I learnt not to waste my energy on what I considered to be 'boy banter'. I left them to it and entered my own sweet world where my opinion mattered. After a while, the sounds of their voices all rolled into one.

Touring with an all-male crew is a lonely and tricky business. It is lonely because the sharing and caring is scarce and double-edged. And tricky because of the man-made rules around flirting, sex and being sexy.

At the venues and after the sound check, the guys would go 'hunting'. They were young and always on the look-out for female attention. The drummer was a handsome man and had his routine of walking round the venue to pick a girl or two for the night. Stand up sex was popular.

One time he said to me,

"Why don't you wear something sexy?"

I had made a point of dressing down, blending in with the boys; most times I wore a T-shirt and trousers outfit, similar to them. His comment alerted me and I mistook his words for attention!

I slipped out of the building and ran to the nearest shop, a corner Indian store. I found a colourful shirt and wore it open at the front and tied in a knot at my waist. It was kind of sexy.

The drummer said, "Nice, darlin'!"

I had no idea what he meant.

The bandleader, who also was the singer, said,

"You shouldn't dress like that. You will bring all kinds of men to our door."

I screwed my face up, as I am sure you are doing now. All kinds of men would come to their door to hustle for me? And remember, they were out on the prowl anyway. Now why would that be a problem? Call it the double standard, or one rule for you and one for me. Was he telling me to dress as if I was not a woman?

Was he suggesting that appearing more feminine and a bit sexy would attract 'bad men'? It was confusing.

The Boys could do the stand-up sex thing where ever they liked and they did. And it seemed the girls loved it too, from the cries of pleasure echoing down the hallways.

But my sexual adventures had to be approved, stamped and agreed upon by the Boys? Now just imagine that scenario!

I stayed with the band for six months, we had paid work and I gained a lot of experience. It was business, not fun. It was a job that paid the bills and the rules were like that. At least I didn't have to wear some ridiculous skimpy outfit, as has been the case in other bands. There was no putting on the glitz, it was just work.

Facing up to the double standard takes some effort as most times men deny its existence fervently. The guys look at you as if you dropped out of planet zonk. The idea that they are treating you differently is bewildering to them. It is so profoundly embedded in their DNA.

Let's face it, it doesn't matter what you wear, someone will always comment. And it seems you just cannot win, whatever you wear. It's too short, too long, you are revealing too much or too little. Too many of us women end up saying we will wear what we want and deal with the fallout later. But we know that doesn't always work out either.

The Modesty Panel is There to Protect You

Women in the corporate world have a special dress code that requires certain feminine indices. It implies that at all times you must appear feminine. But you cannot reveal cleavage, or wear a mini skirt, or a skirt or shirt that is too tight. The definition of feminine is always demure. Not too much of this but enough to show which sex you are. You mustn't attract unwanted attention. And yet, the very dress code itself provokes attention.

As architect, Toon Dreessen, puts it:

"Society encourages all women to wear skirts when trying to look professional and yet unaware the conference organisers are going to sabotage them by making them sit on high stools where the men 'manspread' and the women fiddle with their hemline and bits of paper to cover the gap."

The female uniform may change with the decades, yet the rules of showing, revealing and exposing are somehow always included.

Each profession carries its dress code, written or not. Each situation suggests a dress code to follow. And all these details affect our performance.

People and clients have often asked me, should I wear high heels when speaking in public? Should I use more make-up, should I wear jewellery? But I have never heard of a man asking about his dress code. From Toastmasters to a TEDx talk, men wear what they like and often do not even think about it.

Oh, I can hear men screaming in the background about how they prepare their outfit beforehand. And yes, more men go shopping and more men wear makeup. Yet still, the fact is less attention, commentary and critique is paid to boys and men in public.

I remember watching a young male psychologist give a talk about body language. He wore an un-ironed white shirt tucked into his unordinary jeans and trainers. He moved about the front of the stage and when not demonstrating various forms of body positions and gestures, he had his hands in his pockets.

After the talk, I approached him and asked,

"Why do you have your hands in your pockets? Why do men do that?"

"What are you suggesting?" he replied defensively.

I couldn't help smiling, this is a question I have asked many times and his answer was – typical.

"Well, of course, we are protecting ourselves," he said, gaining his composure. "It's a habit, doesn't mean anything in particular. You have a dirty mind!"

Tempting as it may be to analyse a psychologist, neither his casual dress code and 'habitual' mannerisms, to him and to many people, have any relevance to his performance.

Many women today love to dress up for an occasion and put on the glitz. The fashion industry is worth trillions and most of us indulge in it whether we buy from the local flea market, charity shop or a top designer. We create occasions to dress up and put on a show because we want to look good, we want to be attractive, we want to shine. Our image speaks a thousand sentences. And those sentences are part of our performance.

In the Eyes of the Law

In the eyes of the law, the way a woman dresses can affect the outcome of her case. Still today, the outfit a woman was wearing at the time of a sexual attack or rape often bears more significance than the crime committed upon her.

As a divorce lawyer states, "You think clothes don't make a difference? Try walking into a court in a torn t-shirt and flip-flops. See what happens."

Research today emphasises that, whether we like it or not, or are aware or not it takes less than 10 seconds to make an appraisal about someone according to how they appear.

A lawyer points out that, although it is never fair for someone to judge a book by its cover, or for a jury to judge you by your appearance, if you give them a reason to disbelieve you, they will.

There is also The Halo Effect, also known as the 'physical attractiveness' stereotype and the 'what is beautiful is good' principle.

The Halo Effect, at the most specific level, refers to the habitual tendency of people to rate attractive individuals more favourably - based on their personality traits or characteristics - than they would rate those who are less attractive.

We buy magazines and go window and screen shopping to find out what to wear, how to wear it and what effect it will have on our performance. We are constantly seeking ways to change or improve our appearance.

We believe it will affect our performance and the way we impress others. Because we know innately that it does have an influence on our performance.

We understand on a primal level that how we decorate our faces, our bodies and our words, will affect the responses of those around us. Our appearance has a consequence; our words have a reaction and our gestures provoke responses. At the heart of everything we do, we reveal our performance.

How much or how little attention we pay to putting on the glitz varies from one situation to the next. How we handle the different scenarios, how we react to the attention we receive because of the glitz we are wearing that day depends so much on our mood, our experience, the time of day or night and whether we feel threatened or not.

How can we deflect the attention away from our appearances? Is it by dressing up or down or not caring at all? I don't think so. The no-win situation haunts us too much. The emphasis on appearing sexier, more daring and more appealing, continues to pressurise us too. And the confusion of it all can lead us to believe that it doesn't matter how we put on the glitz or ignore it.

When we get through all that murky water, most of us dress to please ourselves. We also do what Meryl Streep did with her conspicuous jacket. We take the distraction out of the equation. And when that doesn't work we have our words.

We have our voice. Sometimes words of anger, assertive and intimidating, and sometimes we just ignore it all - and exit stage left!

The fact remains that women and girls are still judged by the clothes they wear in court, on the streets and on stage. And women as well as men need to become aware of the damage it causes when judgments and criticisms are made.

We need to check our tongues because once you have thrown out your two cents' worth, once you have spouted your evaluation or your opinion about another woman's appearance, the glitz turns ugly. The glitz becomes negative, base, cheap, disgraceful, and vulgar. And, before you know it, you are in 'she asked for it' territory.

Women carry enough ancestral guilt and social pressure to be thin, ever young, only hairy in certain places and judged as feminine. In our quest to be less judged and accepted for who we are, we also need to be generous and kind to other women:

The tongue has no bones, but it is strong enough to break a heart. Take care of your words, take care of your language.

Anon

CHAPTER TEN: PROFESSIONAL JEALOUSY

Big Emotions

It took me a long time to understand all the indices and outcomes of professional jealousy; to comprehend how someone could deliberately sabotage another person to destroy or shake up his or her career and creative energy.

As they say, jealousy is an emotion we can all experience and feel but what you do with it and how you handle it is the real issue. Most of us know what it is to have that green juice rise up from the bile. We have all experienced some mild form of jealousy. Even from childhood, amongst siblings or other family members.

'Why doesn't Grandma like me?'
'I am so jealous you are going on holiday.'
'I am so jealous you got that red dress, I wanted that one!'

We have all been there. Those little moments of 'I want something that you have.'

But then, what do you do with it? How do you not obsess about the success of another? How do you let go of those twinges of envy? And, most importantly, stop yourself from indulging in acts of revenge?

Winning and Losing

I have been in situations throughout my life where I have seen someone else get the prize and the red dress. I remember when I joined Toastmasters; I was forced to re-learn some of those concepts about winning and losing. I thought my speeches were sensational! I thought that, with my stage experience, I would smash the contests and win top prize every time. It was not the case; yes, I had the confidence and the ability to entertain but my content was lacking.

From my Toastmaster experience, I learnt about the art of listening and evaluation. Listening in a focused way and giving constructive feedback. But I also learnt about what it feels like when you don't win. I had to deal with some tough situations where my audience didn't laugh at my humour, didn't get my jokes and sat in silence at my provocations. A deeper analysis could suggest that women on stage have a tougher time, are dismissed before they speak and judged before they start, etcetera. It still doesn't hide the resentment and jealousy I felt when someone else won the contest.

I had to face up to organisational politics that are the preferences, biases and favouritisms of any group of people, from five to five hundred. It happens, it is a human trait. We prefer and support our comrades, the voices and ideas of those around us. We give our vote to the sound of words we are accustomed to.

I had experienced rejection and the humiliation that followed a few times during those Spoken Word, Performance Poetry days. In the Slam teams, I was picked out as the 'reason' our team didn't win, because my material, my performance wasn't up to standard. I was ridiculed and punished as the culprit who let the team down. I was the loser!

I felt the green bile rise up, accompanied with red anger as I looked at the other poets comparing my work - my stage presence, my whole energy - with them, the winners. A new dis-ease was developing inside of me – Compare-itis, along with a fat dose of professional jealousy.

Singled out as the 'loser', I had to 'fight' back, question the system, and question the judging criteria. I mean if I am to improve and be a credit to my team, I need feedback to grow, surely? It wasn't offered. I recognised that punishment was more satisfying to the ambitious Slam team members than feedback.

I wanted to learn from it and I wanted to win the next time.

So, any envious feelings were dismissed, released and left back in that city. For me, it was important to not let any feelings of jealousy grow. I equated it to coming out of the sea and wiping off the cool, salty water to become dry and warm again. I knew instinctively that allowing jealous feelings to develop would be one big, self-sabotage session. I wanted to win, not revel in revenge.

It is also important to remember that we all have egos, personalities and desires to be accepted, recognised and appreciated. We are human and our need for validation manifests from birth. Our urge to be loved and give love is so primeval that it baffles me why so many modern-day coaches and mentors create courses to prevent it.

And jealousy of the mild kind grows from lack of love and appreciation.

Calming the Green Eyes

When Professional Jealousy slips and slides around like mercury amongst professionals, artists, musicians, sports players, speakers and authors, a hell of sabotage and revenge is released.

Intelligence, energy and integrity are more important factors to one's success than wealth, power or prestige.

Warren Buffett

Unfortunately, in this competitive world, often destructive emotions rise up because a person wants that power, prestige and wealth that you appear to own.

For example, when someone else is chosen to play a solo, read the script, get that TEDx talk, the promotion - but not you. Or someone else from your circle, group or team receives the kudos and/or reward; watch out for the rise of that green-eyed snake.

Have you been there? Have you felt jealousy when your colleague got the credit, merit or medal that you believed could be or even should be yours?

That feeling of being left out is extremely common in life. We have even created new abbreviations and nicknames for it, like FOMO (Fear of Missing Out) and 'compare-itis'. And when jealousy steps into the professional world, a darker kind of resentment and revenge comes to light and you can expect bigger fireworks.

In the re-make of *A Star Is Born*, with Lady Gaga and Bradley Cooper (although all previous three versions of the film reiterate the same emotion), there is a scene when the character played by Lady Gaga, Ally, suggests to Jack, the successful rock star played by Bradley Cooper, that he is jealous because she is being signed up by a big record company and her career is taking off. You can interpret his reactions, his emotions, as jealousy and a recognition of his fading career, and probably a whole host of other scenarios. But Professional Jealousy is strong amongst them.

How do we handle our feelings of jealousy when someone else gets promoted, receives the awards or the first prize? I believe it is a test of our spirit of generosity and our sense of self-respect and respect for others.

In a competitive and fast changing world, where you can go from flavour of the day to the used tea-bag in less than 24 hours, taking Professional Jealousy under your belt or under control is tricky but advisable to accomplish.

When jealousy is thrown in your face, it is hard to take the first solution to calm down, take a deep breath and not respond straightaway. Often, there is cruelty or harsh words accompanying the act of jealousy, which hurt and arouse emotion. The temptation is to spit back, to defend yourself and to show the fire in your belly.

And that can be the very trap waiting for you! I have defended myself in those situations with fast firing bullets of anger and I have also stayed quiet and calm. Experience is a great teacher.

For example, once I had a small part playing music in a theatre show. My task was to play over certain sections of the drama, and to play a Sax solo, a sixteen-bar space to create an atmosphere around the drama, to add to the storyline and express the emotions. All went well until the director arrived with his young girlfriend. A pretty, green-eyed girl. Within days, she started to vent her opinions and her desire to take on a role and then she started vying for mine.

One week before the show was to go on, the director said I was to be replaced by his girlfriend who would sing over the section instead. Everyone was surprised, even more so when she began to sing.

The Alto Sax, the instrument I used for this show, has a sound and a range that is closest to the human voice. This young woman had no experience in how to identify and control the flat and sharp notes of her vocal instrument.

At the first rehearsal, her rendition was so dire that the rest of the cast tittered, giggled and moved their hands to their ears. I stayed calm, believing that as the reaction was unanimous, my position would be re-instated.

Then, after her unique version of singing, she made a dash for me, waving her arms and cursing loudly. Did she believe I was laughing at her? Did she recognise her inadequate vocal ability and therefore, blame me? Slim and petite as she was, my initial reaction was to run. I know how much damage an angry woman can do. And I had my precious (read expensive) saxophone around my neck.

I didn't run but stood my ground, holding firmly onto my instrument, protecting my heart and other vital organs.

Now, I can curse in several languages, a talent I specialise in. It allows me to express fully all emotions. And, unlike the petite songstress in front of me, I did have stage experience and knew how to project my voice. I bellowed back a curse that involved animals and family members in very awkward positions. No one understood, but it sounded rough and tough. I lost my cool, the injustice of her jealous rage got to me. However, the vehement roar from my vocal cage stopped her in her tracks.

Then the director grabbed the 'wannabe' by her arm, shouting at everyone else to leave the rehearsal room, except me, which he indicated with one finger.

He had this strange mixture of anger and calm as he screamed at his acting crew to get out and a gentler tone at this young woman with her claws out. The director came between us (yes - I was saved by a man!). He told her she was an amazing vocalist and stroked and patted her, turning her attention away from me. Her claws sunk back. He winked at me to move on and out.

Most of the actors left the production that day and I did too. It just wasn't worth the hassle even though we had already done four weeks of rehearsal. That's showbiz and that is Professional Jealousy. The show never hit any stage; the little songbird never made a hit record and the director didn't get his name in lights.

The Masculine Overlap Thing

It is interesting to note that male jealousy is often rooted in love and sex. We cannot deny the fact that the hormone testosterone flows into the blood in abundance and for some men, possessiveness and ownership are discharged with it.

There is a puzzling and annoying irony about this topic: in a society where there are still huge unequal opportunities for women, men display extraordinary jealousy. Like those fanning peacocks strutting around demanding the limelight.

I think women are still afraid to call this out, to say it like it is. We have been massaging their egos for centuries. The punishment for not doing so ranges from the subtle - being excluded from the 'Boys Club', always making the coffee etc - to the rampant and dangerous. From being ostracised to rape and violence. It is deeply rooted in the fact that women and girls are still not heard, understood or believed. And that topic I will reveal soon.

I have seen plenty of jealous men acting out. I have also been the reason - the love and sex object - of the fight. For example, when someone in the band wanted a piece of me and I didn't want him to have any of it. But I did share it with someone else. The choice was entirely mine and that independent action called up a pit of green-eyed snakes.

Men will start punch-ups before, during and after a show over jealousy. Once in a group I was touring with, the bandleader put his arm around me, drew me in close and said,

"Don't worry darling, I will protect you from those hyenas."

He wasn't referring to a crowd of male groupies seeking my sexual attention, just a couple of guys wanting to talk to me.

Within an hour, he was offering his body to me. When I refused, he went mad. He was cursing and warning me that I would be raped and that I needed his protection.

I am reminded of the words of Oscar Pistorius during the trial of this once famous athlete.

"I was besotted with her," he said of Reeva Steenkamp, whom he shot and killed.

It is well known that the green associated with jealousy stems from the green of the heart chakra.

Big Female Emotions

One of my first experiences around Professional Jealousy happened while working with a twenty-four-piece all-female Big Band. Into the green-eyed pot went love and sex and it caused huge disruptions.

I can't remember if it was the bass player who was in love with the conga player or the trumpet player with the drummer but when the third person came into that love affair all hell broke loose on stage. Daggers were thrown, bad vibes struck like lightening and, worst of all, beats were missed.

There I was, standing on the other side of the stage in my Sax section, when the trumpets didn't come in at the expected moment. Or I should say, some did - and one didn't. The lead trumpet was spitting fire at the conga player (or the bass player!), who was stretching her neck over to the bass player (or was it the trumpet player?), who was guiltily bowing her head avoiding looking at anyone. That action in turn disrupted the drummer and within seconds it created a cacophony of noise like musical dominoes. We all grinded down with long, sharp notes – then, a vocal battle broke out. The innocent looked around perplexed and the possessed dished the dirt.

Love and sex was at the root of it but it was dragged into our professional world. It was the beginning of the end for the Big Band and many of us were relieved that this was just a dress rehearsal.

For some people, damage equals revenge. Van Morrison sang about this and captured the irrevocable damage that comes from Professional Jealousy:

"Professional jealousy, can bring down a nation
And personal invasion, can ruin a man
Not even his family, will understand what's happening
The price that he's paying, or even the pain"

Lyrics copyright of Sony/ATV music publishing, BMG.

Fire in Your Belly

There will always be situations where someone else will be chosen over you. When talent, merit and personality will have no relevance – it is just the way of the world. But there will be times when a justified protest is necessary. When an injustice, like a poor decision, nepotism, favouritism, sex and/or money get in the way of a choice. That is when the fire in your belly needs to rise up, and hopefully others in your team also recognise it and support you.

When the bandleader let loose a verbal charge of jealous words and threats, my antennae went into red mode. I knew I had to leave the band no matter that there was an incredible tour lined up.

Travelling and working with a jealous person, especially a man, can be a dangerous and distasteful experience. I quit the band with no regrets but I made a new, hard and fast policy that I would never fuck with the people I worked with. In this case, I meant fuck in every sense of the word. But I also made it clear that if I wanted to pick someone out of the audience (or a stray groupie), it was my prerogative to do as I please. This shocked a lot of men; the double standard is still in fashion.

Women often have to fight twice as much in these situations and the stigma of slut and whore prevails. Sometimes the choice between staying in a band, team or workplace where the presence of a green-eyed monster reigns is a tough decision to make.

As Sheryl Sandberg - COO of Facebook, technology executive, author, activist and billionaire - says, 'Put your hand up girl.'

Get used to putting your hand up, setting boundaries and asking for more, asking why and why not? And always start the way you mean to go on, in relationships and at work.

Women are notoriously flexible, which is a great asset, but there are times when you have to stick to your guns.

The signs of Professional Jealousy are a warning for you to stand strong and make choices and change with your head held high. **Always Step Up & Stand Out.**

CHAPTER ELEVEN: TOO HOT TO HANDLE

Tame that Shrew!

Shakespeare wrote *The Taming of the Shrew* between 1590 -1592. And as the title suggests, it was all about taming a woman who was quarrelsome, disobedient and 'too hot to handle'. She was just not wife material. As Katherina admits in Act 2 scene 1,

"If I be waspish, best beware of my sting".

Here was a woman (back then played by a man!) who did not want to be tied down by the constraints of female life and made it clear. But her younger sister, Bianca, could not marry until she was married (another one of those illogical pieces of male logic), and here started all the problems, for both the women and men.

Petruchio, the suitor who comes to Padua, "To wive and thrive as best I may," embarks on various psychological torments to capture Katherina. He prevents her from eating and drinking, until she becomes a desirable, compliant, and obedient bride. Why? Because she was just 'too hot to handle'! This was written as a comedy but it was about a woman who refused to be obedient and how she was punished and forced to marry and be tamed.

The word shrew, although not often used today, has all the significant meanings we have heard before. A shrew is a bitch, fire-eater, battle-axe, dragon and she-devil. The list goes on, but all mean one thing: a woman who is unmanageable, probably difficult, and even dangerous.

The Hot Woman

What does the phrase, 'too hot to handle' conjure up in your mind? Has someone said it to you? Was it a compliment or did it have some other underlying message? Did you feel that it was about your irresistible, sexy appearance, voice or dress? Did it start to lose this interpretation as time progressed? Was it used as a way to say: 'we had a great time but...'

Perhaps it is not said so openly today but disguised in modern language like 'You're just too much', 'Too demanding ', 'Not wife material', 'Aren't you being a bit emotional?' Or the most in vogue, 'Stop over-reacting.' All those phrases can be translated into: You are too hot to handle.

It is an idiom that is used not only in the bedroom, but also in the work environment. Nowadays, the cool calm approach to business is preferred. Outbursts and temper flare-ups happen. But women are told to stop being emotional and over-reacting and men are admired for showing character!

Women in business complain of being interrupted, talked over and having their ideas and inventions stolen right out of their minds. Complaining leads to 'Stop over-reacting, love', loosely translated as 'you are too hot to handle!'

This bias is still extensive and agitating women in the workplace. Women are told to be sweeter, more approachable and friendlier. Translated that means only one thing: don't complain and don't say there's anything you don't like. Don't speak up or ask for more money and, If you don't like it, go work elsewhere – because you are 'too hot to handle!'

Men are not told to be sweet at work. They do not feel obliged to apologise for telling an employer or boss that their services are worth more. They are encouraged to speak up and aren't penalised for agreeing to disagree.

For female bosses, the delicate balance of being soft but not too soft is tested heavily. The female boss who gives orders better find the right tone of voice but the chances of 'Boss bitch' being whispered are high.

Beware, if a sentence starts with "oh, you are hot!", it might not be long before the other four words are added on! Whether you see it as a compliment or abuse or something in between, it is a phrase loaded with meaning.

If it is used to dismiss you from a love affair or an assignment at work and it can have a detrimental effect on your self-esteem and therefore your performance in life.

But what does that phrase and its variations really mean? How is it used to keep women silent, under control or kept in her place?

For Shakespeare and his contemporaries, it was a kind of comic relief, but nevertheless a warning to women to tame it or else! Is it a phrase that dampens your spirit? Does it make you feel that you should quieten down and go back into the shadows? Or maybe it stirs your blood and makes you want to twist and shout and fight back?

In your mind, does 'too hot to handle' refer to a woman's sexual appearance or prowess? Does it suggest she is just too sexy for her own good? Does it make you think you are too upfront? Or that your skirt is too short, your blouse too low, your work is no good or you're not chilled enough?

It is like the word 'bachelor'. When someone says a man is a bachelor, ask yourself honestly, what does it mean? George Clooney was considered a handsome bachelor (or substitute your favourite bachelor man: Idris, Bradley and so on). He was suave, elegant and living the life of Riley.

But when we turn to the female version, the word is' spinster'. Now honestly, ask yourself what image do you have? In the average thesaurus, synonyms for the word spinster include lone woman, old maid and virgin. So, a spinster is a sad and ugly sight, but a bachelor is something to behold?

I admit, I have had a few love affairs and will say I enjoyed 90% of them. Statistic wise that is impressive. But what happens if I speak openly about them? I guarantee assumptions will start bouncing around in minds and mouths as a result of being honest. Clearly, one of those assumptions is I am not wife material and it is a warning to all men.

I am difficult and probably dangerous. Sexy? Yes – but only for one night. It appears we measure a woman's sexual experiences under a different microscope.

Judgements are laid down for both women and men. Both are critiqued for talking openly about their sexual adventures. But think about the judgements aimed only at women; especially those that are 'too hot to handle'. Like the women who cannot be tamed or stand outside of the 'tamed' categories. Women who do not fit the right shape, size or colour that's fashionable in that area or zone of the world.

An Expensive Conversation

Once upon a time, I wrote a story that later became a speech and a party piece. A story that could happen to any woman, in any part of the world, but here it is set in London, in Claridge's Hotel.

The woman, let's call her Sophia, had just been for a job interview. She had presented her abilities and performed well but the decision as to whether to hire her was left in the air. Feeling uncertain, she popped into Claridge's to escape the rain and sit for a moment to reflect on the interview.

At the bar, she ordered a glass of white wine, crossed her lovely legs and sighed. Naturally, she was dressed elegantly, coiffured and made-up to look attractive and professional.

Soon, a man came to stand next to her. He was dark-haired, wearing a designer suit and oozing Chanel Eau de Toilette. He eyed her from the side and said 'good morning' with a deep, sexy accent.

She smiled. He was charming and distracting from the reality that she may not get the job and then how would she pay the bills and the interest on her new car and the holiday she really wanted and needed (rather like anybody would.) And she was in the mood to have a conversation about it.

He invited her to sit with him and waved to the waiter to bring her another glass of wine, as they moved to a table in the middle of the chic bar.

He drank whiskey on the rocks, and Sophia sipped her wine as the conversation bounced back and forth between them with ease. They laughed at times and nodded and sighed as a sign of understanding and empathy between them. The clock ticked and stomachs rumbled.

"Would you join me for lunch?" he asked, his hand reaching across the table in an open manner. "I have a table reserved here in the restaurant. It would be my pleasure," he added. Sophia looked at her watch, simply to delay her answer.
"It is more comfortable in the restaurant, come join me?" he added.

Sophia stood up and then Jacques did.

"Yes, I am hungry!" she said.
They ordered a light meal, clinked their glasses and resumed a congenial and amicable conversation. They discussed art and cinema with intensity. They touched on travel and weather, then onto music and theatre.

Time passed and they both became aware as the silence that fell upon them. It was an awkward moment and they looked at each other blinking and wanting to speak, but remaining silent.

Jacques began. "It has been a pleasure to meet you and to get to know you. I have a room upstairs, a suite. Come and join me for a brandy." It wasn't a question.

Sophia sat back in the chair, wriggling.

Jacques also sat back.

"Of course, I have a little present for you!"

Now it was clear. Sophia smiled; her head titled back peering at him from an angle.

"Of course, if you prefer cash – I can oblige."

Sophia adjusted her necklace.

"Well Jacques, I'm not sure...but..."

"I have dollars," he smiled.

Sophia reached out and put her hand over his.

"You know Jacques, this has been delightful, lovely company and a fine meal but I cannot accompany you upstairs."

"That is a shame. How can I convince you – shall we say 500?"

Sophia kept her hand firmly above and touching his.

"Well, that is excellent. I accept." Sophia paused, inhaled and exhaled. "But Jacques, I am not coming upstairs with you."

Jacques fidgeted but could not release his hand.

"I have spent three and a half hours with you Jacques," Sophia said, and gave a glorious smile. "I think your offer is very generous and correct for the time I have spent with you." Sophia lifted her hand.

Jacques folded his hands together, his elbows on the table and he leaned in. He was about to speak but didn't.

Instead, Jacques sat back and went for his wallet, pulling out a chunk of dollars. It was a large wad.

He slipped the money under the table without counting it and into Sophia's waiting hand. They shuffled back in their seats.

"Well, that was the most expensive conversation I have ever had," he finally said.

"Yes," Sophia said, folding the dollars and popping them into her purse. "Now you know Jacques - assumptions are very expensive."

I like Sophia. She had stepped into Claridge's to have a drink and escape the rain. She wanted to contemplate her next move and reflect on her interview. A human reaction and normal in Western society; men do it often.

Somewhere along the line Jacques made a judgement, one that he followed through with an expectation. There was an assumption that Sophia was in the hotel to work. Work that is highly paid, and the only references needed are, you appear pleasing. She was judged as a whore, call girl, prostitute, and escort. She was a woman in waiting – waiting to offer sex to a man – waiting to play a game – waiting to get paid.

But Sophia is not a stereotype, blow-up doll or in this case, a call girl. Sophia is like you or me. She attended a job interview, she prepared for it by making sure her appearance was pleasant and professional. She behaved as any human would, making conversation with a stranger.

The difference with Sophia is she asked for a reward. She knew and recognised the assumption Jacques had made and decided that talking is just as hard work as having sex, and should be financially compensated.

Was Sophia clever, crafty, experienced and bold? Was she shrewd and heartless or smart and courageous? Was she a bitch and therefore too hot to handle?

Was Jacques a fool, a poor guy or was he deceived? Judgements, assumptions and categories come so easily. We may not say it nowadays because everyone is so politically correct, or we have travelled so much and believe we are familiar with different cultures. But if we are not saying it, we still have these assumptions flying around in our minds and, in some cases, on the tips of our tongues.

Once, at a prestigious Toastmaster event, I got to perform this story, as a 15-minute piece. Afterwards, I had several people come to question if Sophia was me. I smiled and replied, "She's based on all the women I know."

One young woman, who had waited until all curious questions had been asked, told me she thought Sophia was deliberately corrupting poor Jacques.

"Do you think she was flirting with him?" I asked.

"Of course! She accepted the drink, she had lunch with him, she probably seduced him," the adamant twenty-something said.

"And what of Jacques?" I question.

"Well, he's a man, that's how men are."

"Do you think women should know better?"

"Of course! I mean she acted like a ...(hesitation)... pro. So, that is why he treated her like one."

Across gender and generations, the idea still remains that a man can ask a woman to join him in his room and offer money for sex based on the fact she accepts a drink or a meal. Is this how you see it? Women who dress sexily are asking for it? Women who dress sensibly have no desires and women who dress in a frumpy manner will be called frigid or angry?

This scenario carries the stain of 'she asked for it'. Being judged for your choice of clothes, your expressions and gestures and the location you stand in.

We have now heard about numerous episodes from women who have been approached, cajoled and forced into sex by men with power and privilege.

Tarana Burke, who started the #MeToo movement in 2006, talks about this imbalance of power and privilege and how it creates an atmosphere of vulnerability that encourages submission.

But the idea that if you dress, talk or move in a certain way then you are tempting or seducing poor men is utterly ridiculous.

Chill Out Love, Who Do You Think You Are?

Women are supposed to have the same rights as men at work. Yet men who speak their minds, stand up for themselves, and value their own contributions are applauded as leadership material, while women who do the same things are viewed as troublemakers and 'too hot to handle'.

Does the 'Boys' Club' still exist? Is it just covered up with more tinsel and dust? Many women still work in male dominated environments and even when the ratios are more balanced, the concerns are the same.

Trying to simply be heard in the workplace or having your ideas taken seriously and acted upon continues to be amongst the main grievances. But there are a host of other dissatisfactions and injustices arising for women.

For example, are you a sweet girl or a loudmouth? Do you smile, dress neatly and offer to make coffee/tea or do you say, 'It's over there, help yourself and bring me one too."

Are we there to be pleasing and not to make waves? And if we have disabilities, are not white or creamy coloured, what then? What if we don't fit into the stereotype of the 'typical' workplace female? What if we have an accent, wear a headscarf or a tattoo or two? What if we 'appear' sexy?

How do these understated prejudices, assumptions and judgements bear down on your performance ability? Does it cramp your style or make you more rebellious?

Have you ever made a complaint at work about harassment of a sexual, verbal or power-pushed nature? Are you perhaps still reticent to make a formal complaint because of the flack that may come later? Many women do not speak out because they fear their career will be dead-ended. Or worse, be excluded and ostracised to the point they have no other option but to leave. The figures for women making complaints and having something done about it still rank very low. Time to implement the laws then.

The 'too hot to handle' stigma still floats in the air, like a balloon with labels hovering over us. It affects not only our dress code but also our mind code. And in the end, whether we dress up or down, wear more or less, cover or reveal, labels like 'too hot to handle' are directed at women.

From the thousands of cases from all around the world where women are speaking out about sexual harassment and abuse, the implications of this phrase still stifles the air.

Women are considered too hot to handle and men, according to my friend VJ are 'too cold to hold'.

However you feel about this expression and whichever personal experiences are related to this phrase, the consequences, the backlash and the repercussions cause damage.

To lose a friend, lover or your job because this idiom was applied to you diminishes your self-esteem and confidence and ultimately, your ability to perform fully in life.

How can you change this imbalance? What can you do to offset this version of a woman who is speaking up for herself, not ready to take the slack, stick or sanctioning?

What would you say if your partner in love, in work or even in crime said you were 'too hot to handle'?

I can imagine some of you wouldn't care less if you were called 'non-wife material' but the deeper implications are hurtful and for those to whom it does affect, it can certainly reduce your ability to Step Up & Stand Out. In other words, those negative comments can impede you from performing in your unique, authentic way.
Giving it back as good as you get it has sometimes been a tactic for women. Saying 'thank you' when someone flicks an insult at you can dilute a situation.

And I am sure some of you have tried shrugging and ignoring it or coming back with a fast, smart line as in 'touché'. The list of responses goes on and continues to be recycled until we find a way to dissolve that phrase and all other implications and versions of it.

PART FOUR: STEPPING UP AND REALLY STANDING OUT

CHAPTER TWELVE: HEARD, UNDERSTOOD AND BELIEVED

Two Ears, One Mouth

I remember about a year ago in conversation with a group of women, my turn came to express my thoughts and experiences. I said that one of the biggest struggles for women was getting their voices and words heard correctly, understood clearly, and most definitely believed.

One woman turned to me and said, "Are you referring to sexual abuse?'

"No." I replied. "In every area, in every situation, women are not heard clearly, often interrupted or ignored. Their statements are frequently misinterpreted and far too many of us are just not believed when we do speak up."

There was silence, then some nodding and then some murmurs.

It is hard to admit that today in the 21st-century women continue to encounter resistance to their voices, to their rights and to their experiences being expressed and accepted. In turn, this deeply affects the way we present ourselves to the world and inevitably, how we perform.

As Mary Beard states in her highly acclaimed book, *Women and Power*, about the long history of subduing and suppressing female voices,

"We're not simply the victims or dupes of our classical inheritance but classical traditions have provided us with a powerful template for thinking about public speech, and for deciding what counts as good oratory or bad, persuasive or not, and whose speech is to be given space to be heard. And gender is obviously an important part of that mix."

Yet, as we all know (with or without any expensive empirical study presented by male researchers), women in personal settings talk more than men. Not only do we talk more and for longer, but on more personal topics. Somehow in public situations, in meetings and conferences, women talk less.

Research also shows that men tend to talk more than women in business-focused meetings, conferences and panel debates.

Maybe it has something to do with the constant complaints from women about the way they are being talked over, ignored and mansplained. These are everyday experiences for women. It is a common occurrence on TV, radio and at live events that we are often blind to. Our awareness and attention to this imbedded behaviour is nonchalant and superficial at the least.

Does this blind-siding prevent you from speaking? Does it drive you to dampen down, close up and wait? Does it make you feel ineffectual, irrelevant and unnecessary? Many women admit to this even if they fight back, shout out and elbow in. We talk about glass ceilings but sometimes it feels like glass walls.

I know that when I speak up in a clear voice, with well-articulated words, to express an opinion or idea, the responses are often predictable. I am described as bossy, domineering, too opinionated, know-it-all and show-off. These comments slide off the tongues of women as well as men. In fact, in female company it is remarked how confident I am or 'Where did I get that confidence from?' As if I have some extra magic formula.

The idea that women should or must remain quiet, have fewer ideas and certainly not have an opinion is **so** institutionalised, so much part of our DNA that we tend to let it pass.

We allow it to happen and we remain quiet. But the damage is done. The continuing saga about our lack of confidence, doubting our competence and lack of courage, persist in every arena we step into because of this ingrained dogma that women still should be quieter, more demure and less assuming than men.

What Did You Say?

In her book *You Just Don't Understand*, Deborah Tannen shows why women and men can walk away from the same conversation with completely different impressions of what was said. We give different attention, value and meaning when we hear the same words spoken by a woman or a man.

For example, I remember a situation with a band I was working with. We talked about a song that had a riff that just wasn't sounding right. I suggested an alternative motif, even hummed it.

The guys looked at me perplexed and then continued chatting about the song as if I hadn't said a word.

30 minutes later, the bass player said,
'What was that riff you had G.?'

What happened? Didn't they hear me first time round? Perhaps they didn't understand me? Or was it they just didn't consider my offer? What stopped these men from taking on board my sharp and shipshape musical offer?

We are so conditioned to dismissing the voice of a woman, her opinion, her experience, her point of view, it is almost as if she is speaking another language.

Take the word 'no' and observe what happens when it is uttered by a woman. It can mean, 'not now, but soon.' It has been interpreted as a clear 'yes' and some men have also heard the word 'no' as a signal to proceed soon, like in a minute. It seems women and men have not only different interpretations for words but also feel that whatever word is said, it can be changed.

I Don't Believe You!

The Massachusetts senator, Elizabeth Warren, became the first Democratic candidate to formally enter the 2020 presidential race. Discussion about her 'likeability' surfaced almost immediately. Being 'likeable' is code for 'can we accept women intent on power when this has always been a male domain?'

Arwa Mahdawi puts it concisely in her article in *The Guardian*, re the upcoming Democratic elections:

"If it were possible for Warren to be 'likeable', it would only be if she were able to adhere to prevailing ideas of what is appropriate behaviour for her sex – that is, if she were not seeking public office at all."

We still find it hard to believe that a woman is capable and likeable enough to take on a high position in society.

Many still resent the idea of a woman boss, a woman running a company, a woman flying a plane and especially a charismatic, likeable and successful female president.

We are encouraged to put our hands up, to lean in and speak up, but sometimes the predictability of the response holds us back and silences us.

The Deathly Consequence of Disbelief

For me, the most damaging evidence is the number of women who are murdered by their partners, husbands or boyfriends. Where are the reliable statistics, the horror of these crimes are revealed. In the , it is three women every **week**. In the USA, 1,095 women die at the hands of a man every year, that is three women every **day**.

How many of those murders could have been prevented if women's fears – and the brutal, physical evidence about the threat of violence – was believed?

How many women complain and state clearly their fear of physical violence from a partner but are not believed? How many report to the police and social authorities about the threat of violence and are just not believed? Why do we not believe a woman after violence especially of a sexual nature?

And, more to the point, what does a woman (often with children) do when she is threatened with violence and is not believed? Why are women not believed when they report rape? Why are so many rapists given such light sentences?

Why do women not openly talk about the life-changing effects of rape? Is it because they feel they will not be believed and not understood? And when you are not believed, not taken seriously and not offered justice, how does that affect the way you are able to perform authentically? How can you be in this world, be yourself if you are not basically and fundamentally heard, understood and believed?

The Backlash From Speaking Up

The following are all instances of recent backlashes around the world.

There has never been a case quite like it. Professor Christine Blasey Ford accused a Supreme Court Judge of sexual abuse. The assault took place 30 years previously. This disturbed many people because they couldn't understand why she didn't come forward before. Obviously, this was in ancient times when women were heard, understood and believed!! It has become one of the most publicised testaments to not being heard, understood or believed.

Five men in Spain called *La Manada* or 'Wolf Pack' were accused of raping an 18-year-old woman during the Bull Run in Pamplona in 2016. The five men orally, anally and vaginally raped the young woman, filming it and sending it out to their WhatsApp group.

The defence has stated there was no violence involved, therefore making it less of a crime; as of January 2019, these men are out on bail awaiting sentencing.

In the world of non-celebrities, there is still the notion that a woman 'asked for it' or 'her dress was inappropriate' or 'why was she alone at that hour in that place?' And the best of all, 'she was drunk, I thought she said yes.'

When we have Supreme Court Judges, ex- military and ex-police, as in the case in Pamplona, committing crimes of sexual violence, no wonder women have nowhere to find protection, assistance or justice.

In the USA, 600 women are raped every day. In the UK, the numbers are 236 every day. (*White Ribbon report*)

It is also extremely hard to find reliable statistics for rape crimes in China, Korea, the Arab States and many countries of Africa. In fact, it is so severely under-reported that in some countries there are no figures at all.

Why are men raping women and girls? Is it revenge, hatred or privilege or a mixture of all three? Is it to retain dominance and control? Why are there so many incidents of sexual violence against women? Is it because they don't want us to be heard, understood and believed? Is it still part of the 'taming of the shrew' mentality, or the fact we are too hot to handle and therefore need to be downgraded?

Because if this is the case, how can a woman excel, climb through the glass ceiling or build a career based on her skills and talents? How can a woman perform authentically if she is never going to be believed after an assault? Is the continuing acceptance of male violence against women a way of keeping women quiet and afraid to speak out? What needs to happen for this to change?

Anything You Can Do ...

A man's got to do what a man's got to do.
A woman must do what he can't.

Rhonda Hansome, stand-up comedian

Women have been fighting to do all the things that men do for centuries and have now pretty much achieved and accomplished most of them. We have women pilots, neurosurgeons, priests, lawyers and prime ministers. Wherever you look you will find women working, maybe not on the same pay scale but they will be present. We have women working in traditional 'men's roles' in every area and arena. We can see clearly that women are capable of doing anything that men can do.

But what about the men? Are they doing the things we can do? Are they proficient, efficient and competent enough? Are they even willing to do the tasks that we have been assigned and allocated since time began? And how are the men performing? Is there any evidence that women are preventing or stopping men from entering traditional female jobs?

It seems men still like to retain the authority role because with it comes the financial gain and kudos. I am reminded of the underpaid and under-represented midwife, who provides care for the mother for the whole nine-month journey. Then, the male obstetrician arrives on the scene just as the baby is ready to enter the world. The glory is all his.

In the UK, men have been allowed to work as midwives for four decades and yet after all this time, 99.6% of midwives are female. And, in the USA, only 2% of midwives are male. Yet the popularity of men working as gynaecologists has not ceased.

The pay gap between obstetricians/gynecologists and midwives is blatant, with the former receiving double the pay check. Perhaps this is the decisive line for men between choosing a career as a midwife or an obstetrician?

Yours Is Different to Mine But...

The stereotypical codes - that women talk and ask more, and men decide and act more - have to be phased out. We have become obsessed with labels that serve only to limit our progress. Many men today are exhausted with the label of macho man, the pressure to be seen, heard and believed as a strong, unemotional, super-performer. And likewise, for women, the label of housewife, virgin, mother or whore has reached a peak of dissatisfaction and discontent. There is an undeniable rise of the feminine voice, yet the struggle to be heard, understood and believed continues.

Surely every child, woman and man wants to be heard, understood and believed? Isn't it a right of all humans? Because if we are not listening, we cannot understand or believe, and that means what they are saying (or doing) doesn't count and has no value.

Women too need to take more responsibility for their words and actions. Hold up the mirror ladies and learn how to Step Up & Stand Out for yourselves.

As women, we have to speak openly about our experiences. Ditch the shame and feel courageous and say it like it really is. We have been humiliated into silence and told not to 'kiss and tell' and advised to keep it to ourselves. This method has never worked.

When a young woman/actress goes to meet a Mr Harvey Weinstein-type person, that is, a man in a position of offering you fame and fortune, the truth of that encounter must be told, especially if threats of sexual violence are used.

What is it like to be on that casting couch and having to make a split-second decision about your future? When a man like the film mogul says that you can have all the fame and fortune you like but first suck this? What do you do? Do you believe him?

Do you think that you can't win either way and make a run for it? Do you feel like closing your eyes and just doing it? Do you hope you get the part and someone else will recognise your talent at a later date when the film is a box office success?

Learning how to be clearly heard, profoundly understood, so that people will believe you, is easier said than done. Describing the details, letting everyone know what it is like to be in that situation of having to make a split-second decision that could make or break your future, is extraordinarily difficult.

Women are shamed and blamed for telling it like it is. From being frowned upon to exclusion, the punishments are harsh. But speaking up is crucial to change and momentum is gathering, there are excellent teams and supportive organisations in place to give advice and advocacy.

Being heard, understood and believed means standing up for yourself and acting upon the smart decisions you make in order to stand up and face any discrimination or violence. Most of us have had only basic training in decision-making. There is usually someone else who makes the big decisions for us. From our parents to schoolteachers and later in life, the boss at work, our decision-making muscles become weak. Start deciding for yourself. It doesn't mean you have to be selfish, it just means taking yourself into consideration when you say yes or no to someone else's needs.

It means never stop learning and developing from those you genuinely respect and admire. Become knowledgeable and competent in your field. Carry your wisdom with you.

It means admitting and believing in your competence and using that to be courageous in your actions.

It means practising acts of self-belief - because if you don't believe in you, who will?

It means using your courage to express yourself confidently so you can be heard and understood and so that there is no mistake and ambiguity in what you are saying.

It means remembering you don't have to be perfect and you can use your so-called 'vulnerability' as strength.

Understanding that your unique way of presenting yourself, of performing to your very best, is key to having that nourishing and flourishing life you desire.

CHAPTER THIRTEEN: THAT OLD CRACKED GLASSY CEILING

Is It Still There?

Perhaps you have never seen it, maybe you believe it has dissolved or evaporated. Who knows, you may have evidence that it is cracking like summer Arctic ice. But it is there, holding up solidly below the clouds, above every woman and girl's head. It is a glassy and slippery ceiling that is polished, curated, cared for and guarded 24/7.

Women in the Workplace, a 2018 study based on four years of data from 462 companies employing almost 20 million people by Leanin.Org & McKinsey concluded:

"Women are underrepresented at every level, and women of colour are the most underrepresented group of all, lagging behind white men, men of colour, and white women. Women are dramatically outnumbered in senior leadership. Only about 1 in 5 C-suite leaders is a woman, and only 1 in 25 is a woman of colour."

It continues:

"Research shows that we tend to overestimate men's performance and underestimate women's. As a result, men are often hired and promoted based on their potential, while women are often hired and promoted based on their track record."

The slippery, seemingly transparent Glass Ceiling looms above our heads whether we acknowledge it or not. Whether we have brushed off the encounters or blatantly refuse to see it as an obstacle; it exists.

As Hillary Clinton said,

"Although we weren't able to shatter that highest, hardest glass ceiling this time, thanks to you, it's got about 18 million cracks in it."

I have written poems, articles and performed a talk on the topic of the Glass Ceiling and still it hasn't gone away! I have spoken poetically, ranted and raved, showed magnificent defiance and rebelled at every closed door - and still the Glass Ceiling towers above.

Whether you are in the corporate or show-biz world, on the floor or the stage or in fact the casting couch, the resistance to educated, talented and ambitious women to take top positions is still strong.

It seems that the only way to increase the cracks and open up them pearly gates is if **together** – women and men - knock down the walls that support it. The limiting circumstances that the glass ceiling presents has a profound and lasting effect upon our psyche, upon our ability to perform fully. It urges you to play it small, and suggests you are not good enough.

So, let's get cracking and hammering because our performance skills depend on our attitude, our experiences and our stamina to continue doing what we want to do to achieve our dreams, goals and desires.

The Lumpy Casting Couch

There is no glass ceiling; it's really just a thick layer of men.
Laura Liswood – Secretary General Council of Women World Leaders.

'The world is your stage and the stage is performance just watch out for banging your head on that glass ceiling.' This was a piece of advice thrown at me by an irate woman as she stomped out of an audition.

I was also in the audition-waiting hallway. It was a long, narrow space with hard-backed wooden chairs lining one wall. The women sat crossed-legged, spread legged and cross-kneed, fiddling with sheets of paper. I stood against the wall with my saxophone case propped up between my legs.

I was the odd one out, I thought. I wasn't going to be lying on any casting couch having to make snap decisions about whether to open or cross my legs. I thought.

I had even dressed down, more masculine, cockier and chewing gum. I wasn't going to stir up any desires - this was work!

Finally, my turn came and I went in with a masculine swagger and placed my sax on the table. John or Joe (I really cannot remember his name), the man on the other side of the table, squinted as he scanned me up and down.

"How long you been playing then?" he asked.

Bad start, I thought. Would he throw that question out if I didn't have tits? Testosterone was throbbing in my veins now.

"Years," I said.

"So, can you improvise? Can you interpret a dramatic scene?"

"With your guidance - of course," I replied, smiling to cover up my sarcasm.

"You will have to dress differently," he said, looking at somewhere below my neck. "Can't have you looking like a man."

I looked around the room. There were photos on one wall, mostly himself with other men, and I didn't recognise any of them. His assistant, a very slim, teenage-looking woman with long, blond hair, sat at her desk to the left of him. And next to her that frigging leather couch.

There are a million and one stories from the famous to the infamous about sexual harassment, abuse and force upon women.

From temptations of grand fortunes and fame to aggressive coercion, the idea that a woman or girl is available for exploitation is still an easy option for too many men in positions of power and privilege.

Standing up for yourself, putting your foot down or fighting back doesn't always bring the results you want, or thought you could have. I have been kicked out of many bands and theatre shows for doing exactly that and labelled as 'trouble', 'rebel' or 'fucking whore'.

Stepping Up and Standing Out on the topic of rape and sexual harassment doesn't make you a popular girl – amongst women as well as men. The list of insults and put downs I have experienced could fill a book!

As it turned out, I didn't take the job at the theatre company. The 'Joe' behind the desk did not stir my musical imagination and the play had too many half-naked females running around saying nothing. I decided to refuse the part, as I was dreading being asked to play my saxophone in a half-naked state.

I will feel equality has arrived when we can elect to office women who are as incompetent as some of the men who are already there.
Maureen Reagan, daughter of Ronald Reagan

Let's Work Together

There are many enterprising organizations and aspiring online and offline groups that are contending with the prevailing injustices and the suppression of women. Change is inevitable and necessary in order for all of us - women and men - to flourish and perform to the fullest.

Research over several decades indicates that when women and men work together it combines an excellent array of leadership skills.

They say that men tend to be more decisive, bold and confident, and also over-confident. Women, meanwhile, ask questions, seek conversations and are more inclusive. These are all the ingredients for any business to develop and grow successfully.

Working together means zero tolerance of sexist put-downs, interruptions, mansplaining and emotional drama of the stereotypical kind. It means respect for the different skill sets that women and men bring to the decision- making table. It means that the weakest link dogma is deleted and replaced by recognizing individual strengths:

The 'I can do things that you can't do, so let me get on with them, please.' mentality.

John Keyser, founder of Common Sense Leadership and author of the book *Make Way For Women: Men and Women Leading Together Improve Culture and Profits,* which illustrates how men and women lead differently, writes:

"If we can get male leaders with the humility, inner-confidence and self-awareness to understand and accept that women strengthen a company's leadership and heighten morale, then there will be collaboration, not competition or exclusion. Companies that do not embrace this diversity will be left behind and will not flourish in the future!"

Are You Banging Your Head?

Some women say that they only notice the glass ceiling effect when they become mothers. For breast-feeding mothers and those with 1-3 kids of pre-school age, the general complaint is that returning to work lowers the ceiling to an uncomfortable level. Things change. Your priorities as a mother change and very often the conditions at work are not conducive to those first years as a mother.

I am reminded of a friend of mine who would go into the broom cupboard to express milk from her breasts so she could rush out at lunchtime and offer this natural, nourishing supplement to her baby.

Society still has expectations that women will be the primary care-giver, and work at the same time. But the system is heavily stacked against a female executive with a young child. Travelling, and attending the long and drawn out evening meetings, does not fit with a primary care-giver's routine. And although men increasingly want to be part of those early child-rearing years, the stereotypical work conditions make it a tough choice for many of them.

Working mothers talk about the exclusion at work because they are working an 'easy' 3-day week. Their co-workers take the attitude that the working mothers go home to rest and have time off. Some believe shopping, bathing and feeding babies and children/toddlers is a happy-go-lucky job with no side effects.

And many complain that part-time workers do more work for less money. The work is the same as full timers but the hours are shorter and you still have to do the work in the time allocated.

When it comes to early family life, these are real dilemmas for many families. There needs to be less rigidity in upper management, more flexibility on the floor, and a general change in mindset about men and women's traditional roles.

I have written about this topic before but it needs emphasising: those extraordinary years of early motherhood are exactly when women realise just how slippery that glass ceiling is. And, sometimes it is for the first time.

Other poignant issues that come up for women arise when returning to the workplace after ten or more years of childcare at home.

The multi-award-winning TV series, *The Good Wife* – where a trained lawyer, who took ten years out of career to raise her two children, returns to work – explored this scenario brilliantly. She not only faces the sharp shocks of an ever faster-moving and stress-filled business world but her own coming-to-terms with confidence and courage.

And what does a woman do when she reaches 50, or 75? How does the work arena change and challenge her? Women in the film and theatre world talk about the invisibility they experience between the ages of 45 and 70 plus. There are no roles for them they state. Or they become the grandmother, witch, or other kind of monster. An invisible woman is a term used a lot for women after child-rearing age. The image of a woman as not fertile, not attractive – and therefore useless – is deeply entrenched, in women, men and, especially, young people. The glorification of youth still Rules OK.

Is There a Way Round the Glass Ceiling?

Cracking up that glassy ceiling involves you performing with competence, courage and confidence. It means developing an awareness of how it affects all professions in most countries of the world for all stages, ages and races of women.

- It is about making conscious moves
  and not denying its existence.
- It is about courage and learning
  from your mistakes and setbacks.
- It is about confidence and not taking life so seriously.
- It is about competence; and learning more every day.
- It is about developing some smart tactics to disarm your critics.
- And, it is about listening to and empowering other women.

In my speech titled 'Slipping and Sliding on the Glass Ceiling', which I gave at a conference called Entrepreneurial Leaders Live, in Brighton in June 2018, I entertained my audience with the stories of my encounters with the male guards on the glass ceiling entry posts. I had many experiences dealing with these short-sighted wardens who often lacked knowledge, respect and intelligence. I have learned to laugh at many of them and to recognise the ingrained doctrines of female incompetence and the natural superior ability of men that is still rattling around many brains.

I have done the 'rise above it' scenario, the 'ignore them, they know not what they do' habit and the 'what are you doing here with all those clothes on' behaviour.

But experiences are like calories – you can load them onto your hips and carry them around all your life and probably get ill from it all. Or you can shake and shape them into creating a fabulous life for yourself.

I have had a few relationships with glaziers (to find out the tricks of the trade), and they all say 'the best way to shift a heavy and thick glass ceiling is to knock down the walls that hold it up.'

So, readers, knock down them frikkin walls!

CHAPTER FOURTEEN: YOUR PERSONALITY IS YOUR BIZ-NIZ CARD

Where Can I Get Some?

We should take care not to make our intellect our God; it has powerful muscles but no personality.

Albert Einstein

I have encouraged you to tap into your performance skills and make them your indispensable key to achievement and success – in whatever you choose to take on in your life. I have also encouraged you to read the common-sense manual and utilise it as often as possible because this combination is powerful.

There are of course other ingredients to make that cake rise. And one that is crucial is the exclusive mix of your magnetism, aura, experiences, language and physical gestures. It is all the good, bad and ugly that makes you - you. It is your personality. It is your special energy, passion and fire.

And I know some of you are saying,
'Great, but where can buy it? Where can I get some?
'I don't have charisma, I am not like that. I am an introvert!'

Passion has many faces; it doesn't have to be the wild and the 'in yer face' type. It is your original spirit, it is your appeal and allure, and if you think you haven't got it? Well then, you need to start cultivating it and admit you have more of it than you have been told or believed.

Everybody has some attractive quality. Ask around, look in the mirror, record a video. Become friends with yourself and you will find your charm. Your personality is what people buy; it is the big attraction, the attention puller and the lifeblood of your performance.

And as you now know how to shake off the inhibitions and you understand the negative impact of labelling yourself, you then appreciate that when you perform authentically, the world sits at your table. You will be able to convert, shift and spin this knowledge and wisdom to give you access, permission and direction to release your sweet personality.

Don't Take Yourself Too Seriously. There is a Life After Mistakes.

Everybody wants to be liked and almost everybody (at some time in their life) wants to be funny. Funny equals popular and humour has a special ability to uplift and create connections. No one can deny the healing benefits of medicinal laughter.

If you check out your favourite comedy show or personality, the majority of their material comes from the mistakes they have made or those of their family or friends. Good humour is about laughing at the errors, foibles and faux pas that we produce accidently, intentionally or through divine intervention.

We humans have been making a whole pile of ridiculous and horrendous mistakes for centuries. All too often we become caught up in moral and religious codes: we become focused on division instead of what we have in common. We lose sense of what life is about.

A common malaise of this fast spinning 21st -century world is how many of us just take ourselves far too seriously. That is the inability to see the lighter side, a humorous angle or a flexible alternative. This is the slippery slope to trouble and strife, the prelude to warmongering, divorce and hatred.

We become tight, moody and grumpy and, at worst, nasty and vengeful. Admitting you are not perfect, not right, or faulty in any way, can cause a war, can cause a wall to be built.

Let's face it, at the root of it all, when we break it down to the core of our souls - we want to be liked! It is nothing more than a simple human need to be liked, appreciated and admired. And why not? If you have talent, something to show or share, the desire for a response is normal and healthy. The majority of us have been displaying this need since childhood. We all seek approval, another normal human element. We find the balance by learning from each other's and our own mistakes.

Throughout my life, I have had to battle with whether I could or should reveal my personality or not.
I was considered:
Too much
Too hot to handle
Too opinionated (too bossy)
Too know-it-all
Too smart (arse)
Too complicated
Too sexy
Not sexy enough
Too tough
Too mouthy

I was most definitely a 'couldn't please all the people all the time' kinda girl. I was the rebel with too many causes and far too wayward and forward. I have never had a 9 to 5 job; oh wait, I did: I lasted 2 hours. I believed that life is about selling what you've got and I sold it all. Your personality is what makes you rich. I learned, from an early age, to believe in the Lighten Up and Live Longer method. Sometimes I excelled and a few times I just couldn't laugh myself out of the mess (that I'd often put myself in).

Finding a harmonious balance between being liked and appreciated and not doing the pleasing everybody shuffle is a slippery manoeuvre for everyone. Be reasonable and don't be harsh on yourself; it is a lifetime skill to learn and to negotiate.

Don't take life so seriously. You will never get out of it alive.
Elbert Hubbard - philosopher and writer.

Take a Pause on the Wild Side

When you learn another language or are faced with a strange accent or dialect, don't you wish that person would talk slower? Even just to pause for a moment. And again, when a TV presenter, a speaker, even your doctor starts talking like a fast train to nowhere, you just want them to take a break and breathe. Sometimes, you wish you could just press their pause button.

The 'silence is golden' formula is the magic of any speech, pitch or performance. Timing is everything. In the written word there is punctuation and in the spoken word we have pauses. The pause is an oral comma.

When you insert the pause in the right place, it can create a buzz of excitement and a moment of awareness. It allows for breath, for understanding, for emotion, laughter or tears. It creates a space to ponder and think. It arouses empathy.

The pause gives you authority and respect. Pausing exudes confidence and it shows you are in charge. Of course, it works best when you are well rehearsed, when you know your lines, your moves and steps. Then you can control the pace and the measure. You can let your words sink in, and really observe a reaction in your audience, the listener or the person in front of you.

Pausing on a bigger scale has its own rewards and benefits, from a night off to a weekend away or even a cruise around the equator! Taking a break from your workload and routines is the place to re-generate the brain cells, revive your energy and restore your vision.

Whenever you find yourself on the side of the majority,
it is time to pause and reflect.

Mark Twain

Do It For Me One More Time

I remember those long hours of running the scales up and down on my saxophone. Learning fluency, dexterity and agility. Working the muscles on my mouth to form a solid embouchure to produce the sweetest sounds.

I remember all those days repeating the lines from my speeches, poems and plays, so I could give them meaning and expression. Time dedicated to learn the words, to find the places to stop and pause, to move and add gestures.

At the time, I had to inject discipline and focus into my mind to hold back the distractions and the 'wish I was out playing with my friends' craving.

One of the best ways to improve your performance and start to exude more personality is through rehearsals. Call it repeated actions, a revision, try-out, workout, drill, prep or dry run - it is all the same.

It is you improving your performance. You can name it as warm up, work out, review, experiment, honing or run through; it is all about you tuning up your instrument of communication, getting it ready for your connection, your unique performance to the world, or to whomever. And during this invaluable, educational learning workout, you will locate and acknowledge your personality.

Sounds crazy, feels like a school lesson? Believe you can wing it? One way to understand the wonders of rehearsals is to imagine someone you admire who wants to see and hear you – and then says,

"Do it for me one more time."

For writers, rehearsals take place in the editing suite. The room where you sculpt, snip and cut up your words and sentences until they are smooth and shiny and your editor is smiling from ear to ear.

When I am learning a speech, I start by reading it over and over again. I read it out loud to hear the words, the vocabulary. Are the verbs doing their thing in an exciting way? Are the adjectives at the perfect temperature? Is the sentence too short or too long? By reading out loud, you hear what works and what doesn't gel.

As you repeat this process, you begin to insert colloquial phrases, you liven up the fill in words and you jazz up the structure. It is the evolution of your speech, pitch or piece. The rehearsal is when you add all the bits and bytes that illustrates and radiates your personality.

Rehearsal and practice is about repetition and we all do it, every day. Do you recall the first time you wrote your first poem, song or business presentation? Were you able to express yourself fully with confidence and competence?

Did you think it needed a bit more of something? Could you have taken it up a notch if you had gone over it a few more times?

You have to rehearse many times in your life, so find a style that suits you, and get practicing your skills and crafts. Develop your performance. So every time you open your mouth, you offer the best performance.

Practice makes you proud and practice makes a performance.

Get a Life! Wakey-Wakey!

Why not focus on what you have instead of making lists of what you don't have?

Far too often we are dragged down by words and images from TV, radio, advertising, our colleagues and partners, and become immersed in negative experiences. Every hour you hear the news of doom and disaster, no hope and terrible loss. It can drive you to Hotel Pessimistic.

It can cloud your mind, delete and annul all the good intentions you have for living a nourishing and flourishing life.

So, Get a life, wakey-wakey. Make a change, jump off the Con Belt. Leave the man! You do have a choice.

I am not referring to praying for a miracle or wishing on a star or any abracadabra. You know you have to take action, do some forging, shaping and designing. But first you have to get a life.

We all have obligations that can limit us. The economic ones, health and family are the most familiar dutiful acts we have to deal with. Just don't use any of them as a reason or an excuse to stop you from achieving your dreams, goals and passions.

Of course, it is not easy. If you want easy you are reading the wrong book, living on another planet. Easy does not challenge or teach you anything. And ask around, easy is boring.

You have to Step Up & Stand Out, fight for your rights and search for the answers. And your personality will start pricking its way out of your body and soul. You might feel itchy, restless and driven. That's good, that's fire and passion and a guarantee it will start your engine running.

People may hear your words, but feel your attitude.
John C. Maxwell

Curiosity Doesn't Kill Cats, It Opens Doors

When did you stop asking why, why and why? What happened to your inquiring mind? When did it switch off? That thirst to know and understand more, to open up a box of truths, secrets and lies, of facts, opinions and ideas. That feeling of getting under the skin of a topic and sinking your teeth into it.

It's called 'asking'.

Asking has become a complex option that still many of us obsess about. Is the act of asking a strength or a weakness? Does it signify you are dumb, ignorant or too lazy to look it up for yourself? Is it something that reveals you are not in control and therefore displays chinks, gaps and holes?

Sheryl Sandberg - COO of Facebook, technology executive, author, activist and billionaire - has encouraged us to Lean In and put our hand up. I take that one step further, to open your mouth and ask. Remember the abyss of over-thinking and over- worrying what anyone is going to think about you? This is the time to lose that concept and let it hang over someone else's shoulders.

Laughter is a good thing, right? And anyway, you now know how to deal with hecklers. Go give it back. Don't let anyone sneer, snigger or scoff at you. You've got personality.

I always tell myself that it is a great relief there are people who know more than I do. Because I do not know everything, I keep my childlike and adult-styled curiosity in plain sight. I hold those five provocative words of Why? Where? When? What? How? at my fingertips, ready to catapult out whenever I need them.

Asking is a strength and it shows courage and character. These are all vital ingredients of your personality that will make you even more memorable. Asking questions will take you everywhere!

As the businessman and entrepreneur Sam Walton says: "Curiosity doesn't kill the cat, it kills the competition."

Disarming Your Critics

It was on the second night of the theatre show I wrote, produced and ended up acting in (don't ask but there was more drama off stage than on). It involved gruelling hours, heated rehearsals and plenty of vitamins. But the show goes on regardless.

I was exhausted from all the roles I had taken on and I was close to letting off steam, venting my anger and going off the rails.

After that second night when things were still shaky and unsettled, a woman came up to me in the bar and started waving her finger at me telling me what a load of rubbish the play was and wasn't I ashamed to put it on!

Now, I could have easily drawn my sword and sliced off the top of her ponytail, but I didn't. Out of my mouth came the most soothing sound:

"Thanks for coming to the show, I appreciate your comments."

Impressive, right? She stood there with her mouth open; I could almost see the bile rising up in her. She walked away, and I exhaled.

I had disarmed my critic.

I still relish that moment that display of cool, calm and refreshingly delicious comeback. I can only recommend utilizing this method as often as you can. As often as you can, control anger, frustration, injustice, fury, inequality and offence.

It takes courage to stand up to negative criticism, especially if it is not followed up with something constructive. No one benefits from total annihilation of their work. We all need encouragement, feedback and recommendations as to how to improve. That's how you learn and find out what you are made of, or how you affirm your personality.

In the wise words of Danielle LaPorte,
"It's more important for you to believe in your powers of discernment than someone's healing powers."

Smiling with Your Elbows

Body language is the linguistic queen of expression.

I recently watched a video of Marcel Marceau, who truly mastered the art of performing without words. He called his mime 'the art of silence.' But what he expressed instead was all the emotion, passion and vocabulary with his face, hands and body.

We are all experts in reading the expressions of our children, loved ones and even our bosses. We understand clearly what that raised eyebrow means, that squinting of the eyes and that twitching of the lips, not to mention that wagging finger.

We have learned to interpret many gestures and physical movements and adapted some ourselves. But when it comes to communicating your message, idea or opinion, there is nothing like a little body language to emphasise and describe your meaning to a fuller extent.

There are unspoken rules and guidelines about physical contact with people you don't know: how close to stand, when to touch and what to touch. The codes and protocol vary according to rank, gender and culture.

In cultures/countries where people kiss on greeting each other, offering a hand is considered formal. Some businessmen will kiss and grab each other's shoulders, the French and Russians for example. In the corporate environment, touching women on the knee, neck or elbow can be considered as crossing a dangerous line. Where formality counts and is important and you want in on a project, don't mess with their rules.

Otherwise, let your body do some talking. Let yourself be free with expressing your personality in a physical manner. Practice the power standing position, smile with your eyes, take your hands out of your pockets and let them say a few words.

Nowadays it is easy to watch a video with no sound as so many have subtitles. How does that speaker use their body to enhance the story they are telling? And combining body lingo with pausing creates a riveting reaction worth imitating.

It is true many people still carry inhibitions about taking up space or, more accurately, other people's space. Women are good at apologizing for stepping in and up. Well, no wonder with all the rules and regulations that have been in place about the 'position' of women in society. As I have said before, it is time to stop worrying about what other people think. Change your mindset, change your thinking or switch off the commentary, but do something about it, so you can let your body, your face and your hands say more about and for you.

When your personality is asking to be released, there is nothing like a bit of body language, it is your personal weapon of expression. Becoming more confident through learning and experience and through practicing your art or craft gives you the impetus you need to add more, show more of your original personality. It is your style of doing and moving.

All Together Now

Performing with personality is at the root of it all. And knowing yourself, with all your strengths and weaknesses, all your highs and lows and the unpolished bits in between, is the adventure you - and only you - can discover. It involves:

Learning to laugh and accept your mistakes and move on from them.

Taking a pause with your words and actions, as it encourages confidence and a sense of you being in control.

Recognizing the process of rehearsals and repetition as an excursion full of adventure and discovery.

Be curious, take up space and ask. Stop imagining the 'worst scenarios', stop thinking about what if and what not - life is much shorter than you realise.

Everyone catches up with their grandmother and you will too. So ask and be curious.

Find the best way to ignore negative chatter, criticisms and opinions. Disarm them by not rising or responding in a predictable way.

Have some fun with your body. Relax those shoulders and hands and make some funny faces. Don't take yourself so seriously!

All of these skills are interrelated and connected to you, your personality and your way of performing. Some will enhance your expressions and some will come more easily than others. I am sure you will discover you already have oodles of these skills and just needed to read that you are on the right path. We all need attention and approval, it is healthy; we are social creatures.

Step Up & Stand Out. Tell and Demonstrate, to the world and the people you care for, that you have personality, and you are going to show it (expose) and perform, to have that Nourishing and Flourishing life you richly and rightly deserve.

APPENDICES

BIBLIOGRAPHY and REFERENCES

Chapter 1

I want to be authentic

a.) https://www.europeaninterest.eu/article/womens-capacities-not-used-full/

b.) Gender pay gap UK in 2016, according to Eurostat
https://ec.europa.eu/eurostat/documents/2995521/8718272/3-07032018-BP-EN.pdf/fb402341-e7fd-42b8-a7cc-4e33587d79aa

c.) Věra Jourová quote
https://www.europeaninterest.eu/article/womens-capacities-not-used-full/

d.) Billboard 100 list
https://www.billboard.com/articles/business/6874816/billboards-2016-power-100-list-revealed

e.) Lack of women in music industry
https://www.hypebot.com/hypebot/2018/01/billboards-mostly-male-power-100-confirms-women-in-music-study.html

https://www.nytimes.com/2018/01/25/arts/music/music-industry-gender-study-women-artists-producers.html

f.) Economist Sylvia Ann Hewlett
http://30percentclub.org/wp-content/uploads/2014/08/The-Sponsor-Effect.pdf

Chapter 2

Using performance to escape the con belt

a.) Mary Beard, *Women & Power: A Manifesto*, Profile Books, 2017, from the preface

b.) Miss Triggs cartoon, downloadable for free here: https://www.flickr.com/photos/24736216@N07/8557079931

c.) Mary Beard, *Women & Power: A Manifesto*, Profile Books, 2017 quote from Homer, page 4

d.) Yuval Noah Harari, *Sapiens, a Brief History of Mankind*, Vintage, 2015 - Chapter 6, pages 126/127

e.) Women bank accounts 1975 https://www.moneysupermarket.com/credit-cards/womens-financial-rights/

f.) Financial Times, April 2018 https://ig.ft.com/gender-pay-gap-UK/

g.) Original meaning of awesome https://en.oxforddictionaries.com/definition/awesome

h.) Katty Kay and Claire Shipman, *The Confidence Code*, HarperCollins, 2014, page 5 - Mike Thibault

i.) Katty Kay and Claire Shipman, *The Confidence Code*, HarperCollins 2014, page 12
Christine Lagarde, who runs the International Monetary Fund, admitted to the authors that she "zealously-over prepares for everything."

Chapter 3

All you need now is - the confusing world of advisors, coaches and mentors

a.) Katty Kay and Claire Shipman, *The Confidence Code*, HarperCollins 2014, page 12, Christine Lagarde

b.) Katty Kay & Claire Shipman, *The Confidence Code*, HarperCollins 2014, page 13,
"The shortage of female confidence…"

Chapter 4
Having a professional mindset and all that jazz

a.) Tower Theatre
http://www.towertheatre.org.uk/

b.) Carla Marie Williams
https://www.theguardian.com/music/2018/mar/08/music-industry-still-boys-club-beyonce-songwriter-carla-marie-williams

Chapter 5
The Four Fabulous Sisters

a.) Ian Jack article on Charles Dickens
https://www.theguardian.com/commentisfree/2019/feb/23/charles-dickens-wife-victorian-asylum

b.) Jean Nidetch
https://www.britannica.com/biography/Jean-Nidetch

Chapter 6
How to get your mojo back

a.) Whore of Babylon
https://en.wikipedia.org/wiki/Whore_of_Babylon

Chapter 7
Carving out your place in a world full of words

a.) Julia Gillard interview.
https://www.ft.com/content/6c08ca36-7b70-11e8-af48-190d103e32a4

b.) Mary Beard, *Women & Power: A Manifesto*, Profile Books, 2017

c.) Carol Ann Duffy
https://en.wikipedia.org/wiki/Carol_Ann_Duffy

d.) Lucy Crompton-Reid
http://applesandsnakesblog.org/
blog/a-fond-farewell-from-lucy-crompton-reid

e.) British journalism quote
https://www.theguardian.com/media-network/2016/
mar/24/british-journalism-diversity-white-female-male-
survey

f.) Carrie Gracie quote
https://www.theguardian.com/media/2018/nov/17/carrie-
gracie-bbc-gender-pay-gap

Chapter 8

The twice as good scenario

a.) Jennifer Coates, linguist
https://aggslanguage.wordpress.com/2009/10/06/jennifer-
coates-subculture-and-conversational-style/

b.) Julia Pascal
https://www.theguardian.com/commentisfree/2018/
apr/24/women-theatre-quotas-stage-gender

c.) Airline pilots
https://centreforaviation.com/analysis/reports/women-
airline-pilots-a-tiny-percentage-and-only-growing-
slowly-432247

d.) British Law society figures
https://www.lawsociety.org.uk/support-services/practice-
management/diversity-inclusion/articles/statistics-show-
women-still-under-represented-in-the-judiciary/

e.) Number of women CEOs at Fortune 500
http://fortune.com/2018/05/21/women-
fortune-500-2018/

f.) Male teachers
https://www.bbc.com/news/education-37552056

g.) Female barrister insult
https://www.legalcheek.com/2019/02/more-action-needed-to-tackle-hostile-environment-driving-women-from-the-bar/

h.) Women voting rights in 12 countries
https://theconversation.com/womens-votes-six-amazing-facts-from-around-the-world-91196

https://www.quora.com/In-which-countries-do-women-not-have-a-right-to-vote

Chapter 9
Putting on the Glitz

a.) Toon Dreessen article
https://www.architectsdca.com/panel-discussions-focus-on-the-table-skirt-not-the-womans-skirt/

b.) The Halo effect
https://www.verywellmind.com/what-is-the-halo-effect-2795906

Chapter 10
Professional Jealousy

Van Morrison lyrics for the song Professional Jealousy
https://genius.com/Van-morrison-professional-jealousy-lyrics

Chapter 11
Too Hot to handle

a.) The word spinster
https://www.merriam-webster.com/words-at-play/spinster-meaning-origin

Chapter 12

Heard, understood and believed

a.) Mary Beard, *Women & Power:
A Manifesto*, Profile Books, 2017
"Again, we're not simply the victims", page 21.

b.) Deborah Tannen, *You Just Don't Understand*,
Virago, paperback, 1992
http://time.com/4837536/do-women-really-talk-more/

c.) Arwa Mahdawi Guardian article about Elizabeth Warren
https://www.theguardian.com/commentisfree/2019/
jan/03/elizabeth-warren-likability-us-media-sexist-
hillary-clinton

d.) Number of women murdered in UK
https://www.theguardian.com/commentisfree/2018/
dec/18/women-uk-femicide-statistics-died-male-violence

e.) La Manada Wolfpack Latest news January 2019
https://www.euroweeklynews.com/2019/01/03/the-wolf-
pack-court-rules-la-manada-men-can-remain-on-bail-
ahead-of-sex-assault-appeal/#.XKG-I2QzaE8

f.) White Ribbon report PDF
https://static1.squarespace.com/
static/5965f0e9e58c62e0520e1d7b/t/5a37ac3aec212d3
032424e4b/1513598011028/UK+Facts+and+Figures+-
+Violence+Against+Women+and+Girls.pdf

g.) Male midwives
https://www.bbc.com/news/magazine-41426691

Chapter 13

That old cracked glassy ceiling

a.) Women in the workplace study 2018
https://womenintheworkplace.com/

b.) John Keyser, founder of Common Sense Leadership
and author of the book *Make Way For Women: Men and
Women Leading Together Improve Culture and Profits*,
Librastream, 2015
https://www.entitymag.com/collaborate-men-and-women-
in-the-workplace/

Chapter 14

Your personality is your biz-niz card

a.) Marcel Marceau video
https://www.youtube.com/watch?v=XEsfpRrfXf4

ABOUT THE AUTHOR

Georgia Varjas is a multi-skilled artist who lives in Spain. She has
worked as a saxophonist, playwright, performance poet, author,
blogger and speaker. She has won Poetry Slam Contests in the
UK & the US.

Listed below are plays, poems and stories that Georgia has
written, performed or published.

- *CC's Agenda* - written by Georgia Varja
  Performed at Canal Café Theatre,
  London 27th April - 1st May 1999

- *Blood Sisters* – A play written by Georgia Varjas -
  directed by Howard Whiteson –
  produced by Virtual Vixens Theatre Company

  Performed at Hackney Empire Studio Theatre, London.
  11th Jan – 22nd Jan 2000

- Words On the Wild Side – Georgia Varjas -
  A Poetry Collection – Create Space USA – 2011

- Divine Damages – Georgia Varjas Short Story Collection
  - Create Space USA - 2013

- Story entry in three anthologies:
  Talk of the Town - Wordplay Publishing – 2014
  Leaping into Christmas – Wordplay Publishing - 2016
  The Book of Inspiration – Busybird Publishing 2017

This book is a female account and exposé of life in the fast and slow lanes of show-biz, the arts and anything on video, stage or page.

It also demonstrates what it feels like to slip, slide and bang your head on that old cracked glassy ceiling. A friendly glazier told me that the best way to break a heavy glass ceiling is to knock down the walls that hold it up.

Dear reader, this book does just that...